Masticate and Swallow
A Cuban-American Childhood

Fabio Alberto Hurtado

t

Término Editorial

Editor: Roberto Madrigal and Stephen Wildfeuer
Design: Kistin Jordan (Kistin Creative Studio)
Cover photograph: Rebecca Hurtado © 2017
Cover design: Kistin Jordan

Termino Editorial
P.O. Box 8405
Cincinnati, Ohio 45208

Library of Congress Cataloguing-in-Publication Data

Hurtado, Fabio Alberto
Masticate and Swallow: A Cuban-American Childhood
ISBN-13: 978-0930549541
ISBN-10: 0930549546

Library of Congress Control Number: 2017919135

Termino Editorial, Cincinnati, OH

to all my children and grandchildren,
who made me want to write this story
and
for my parents and grandparents
who will love reading this book

CONTENTS

PREFACE

*"There is nothing to **writing**. All you do is sit
down at a typewriter and bleed."*
Ernest Hemingway

About a decade ago, I started writing this collection of stories you are about to read. I wanted to write about my Cuban childhood. The passing of time has helped me understand that I want to write about Cuba only to the extent that I can tell you about my family.

I was one of ten million people living in Cuba in the 1970s. And the first part of this story takes place in La Habana, Cuba's capital. In September 1980, my mother and I flew to Costa Rica and lived there for three months and three days; then we moved to Elizabeth, New Jersey. I did that as a ten-year-old boy while knowing one English word: *cowboy*. The second part of the story takes place in Elizabeth in the mid-1980s.

I was born in Havana in a neighborhood hospital in what was considered the suburbs of the city, prior to Fidel Castro's 1959 Revolution. In the 1970s, I grew up in the Lawton and Vibora Park neighborhoods. I split my time between my stepdad's (Tan) house and my grandparents' house, where my father lived. I spent weekdays in Lawton and weekends in my grandparents' house in Vibora Park. My grandparents are one of the reasons I need to tell this story.

I also want to tell it because I am the last Cuban-born person in our family; if I do not tell it, our family will forget it. Like in most stories, there are sad parts. Life could be hard in Cuba. There are funny parts, the neighborhood man who ate glass; and there are weird parts, the being naked in the park, or the stealing of food in New Jersey. And then there are the parts where I can now look back and see experiences preparing me for a future, in a country, I could never predict.

All the parts are true parts. I am not writing this story to be a writer of fiction – I gave that up. The only way to motivate myself to finish this story was to write it *for my children and grandchildren* and to think of it as a gift only I can give them: my truth about my childhood and why we left

Cuba, what we lost there, and what we gained in coming to the United States. The faith I have is that you will read it and you will make more out of it and with it than I can ever imagine. And that in it, my family will feel the love of a father, and will hear, from the past, the voices of their Cuban family.

(Concord, North Carolina, October 2017)

Part I: La Habana

TE-TE, VA-CA

I don't have a personal memory of that morning when my mother quickly packed a small bag, placing the cloth diapers and the pacifier near the bottom, and a thermos of Cuban coffee near the top. I've been told there was an argument – later there would be more. My father was having an affair. In a country where men casually have affairs, the women – expected to ignore them – follow a tradition of silence. My grandfather had an affair, and his father, all the way back to the first Spaniard fathers guarding the city from English pirates. A way of life. Piracy and affairs. Not so different really. That was the traditional view. Unluckily for my father, my mom was willful, independent, and feisty, not at all the traditional middle-class Cuban bride. He liked her independence while they dated, but it got in the way of his traditional domestic expectations.

My mother, who had been catching buses since my birth as a tactic to make me sleepy, hopped on the first bus passing through *La Calzada de 10 de Octubre* that morning. She boarded toward Guanabo Beach, on the outskirts of Havana. She was not picky about a destination. I don't picture her crying. As a boy, I could never picture my mother crying. That changed later.

Half an hour into the route the bus made its way through farmland just east of Havana. Cows and palm trees dotted the tropical landscape. I sat on her lap, window side, looking out and feeling the wind. No AC in Cuban buses. "Va-ca," I said.

"Yes, yes, that's a cow, son. *Vaca. Mira.* Another *vaca.* And another." She replied.

"Va-ca," I yelled while a sweaty black man swatted a fly from his forehead with a once white, now yellow handkerchief. I was so excited -- and she more so, because although her life was difficult and her husband was a cheater, her son could say cow in Spanish and that changes a mother's universe.

"Va-ca," I said and pitched my pacifier out the bus window. I beamed a smile of pure love. The cow needed it. "Te-te", I said, and my mother was paralyzed. Her last pacifier had been thrown to a cow by her darling curly

3

blond-haired cherub, who could not understand that in a Communist country a *te-te* is a commodity. Like you need cow dung in Cuba when you are making home-made liquor, you need a *te-te* when you are raising a child. It's a necessity, pure and simple. That was the last of the half-dozen pacifiers she bought from a Czechoslovakian student whom she tutored. Foreigners had unlimited access to pacifiers. When could she hope to buy another one? Not now on a bus to Guanabo. Maybe not ever.

No more *te-te* for you she thought half-cocked, preparing for my tantrum. To take a Cuban child's *te-te* before the age of three or four or seven was unheard of. What would my grandmother and my grandaunts say? They'd say plenty and my mom would have to hear all of it. "What kind of a way is that to raise a child without a *te-te*? Don't bother giving him milk now, either." Very traditional.

My mom's thoughts raced as I kept repeating "Te-te Va-ca" so happily and so innocently. Yes, my darling, the *va-ca* now has a *te-te* and you are such a good loving boy, such a kind soul so concerned over a cow and her need for a pacifier. This social justice angle played well in my family.

After sitting for hours in a small open-air cafeteria that served only lemonade, we boarded the second bus back from Guanabo. I looked at my mom and out the window once again.

"Te-te?" I looked up at her.

She calmly replied "Va-ca," without having to explain why I could no longer use a pacifier, how it would ruin my teeth, how I was getting too old, how she could not just buy one because we lived in Cuba where pacifiers were luxury items. These thoughts on the bus ride mingled with her resolve not to be a traditional wife sitting at home sorting rice and smelling her cheating husband coming home with just a lingering hint of perfume.

"Te-te?"

"Va-ca."

The logic was devastating. I wanted my pacifier; I had thrown it willingly to the cow. How could I pitch a fit? We had a *te-te-va-ca* exchange which she kept winning with the one-word response. "*Va-ca.*" Sometimes problems just fix themselves, thought my mother, all the way back to my grandparents' house in La Vibora. No need to get into a argument trying to convince and cajole her way with her son through the pacifier issue. She thought of the loss and disappointment of young love. She thought of my grandparents' marriage, of her love for her son, and of a cow in a field near Guanabo Beach with a *te-te* in her mouth, waiting for my mother to pack her bags.

TAKING BUS # 1

Shortly after I gave my pacifier away, we moved out of my grandparents' house. Then two years passed when I was just too young to know what passed. One morning when I was about four, my mom told me we were visiting a family friend. I was old enough, I remember, to find strange that we carried suitcases and boxes with us as we visited.

"We are visiting for a day. Maybe two," said my mother.

After the third day, I remember asking mom when we were leaving these relatives; we never did. And so we began life with people who weren't really relatives and shortly thereafter my mother married one of them. My new stepfather, Jorge Posada, loved baseball and books, old movies, and John Lennon, and the Beatles, and long hair. With him I watched Charlie Chaplin and Marx Brothers movies, from him I learned to throw a baseball and jump from a ledge. I began to call him Tan because that is what my (now) cousin Sara called him and she was about my age when I moved to Lawton. He lived in the Lawton neighborhood of La Habana at #95 Lawton Street with his mother, his grandmother, his great-Aunt Nenita, who was a hunchback, his brother and sister in law, and their three kids.

The house is still there between Pocito and Tejar Street on Lawton Street right across from the *Círculo Infantil*, a large neighborhood government-run daycare. This was a small old building on an entire block, with mostly uncared for and overgrown yards. Two blocks down towards Dolores Street was a small corner park we often used to go as kids to play marbles or ride bikes.

The concept of a nuclear family – so seemingly right and orderly and so American – was absolutely alien to Cuba and still is today. The trauma of moving into a house with nine people had more to do with who I was when I got there than with the number of new relatives with whom I had to now share a house. I arrived at this house a bed-wetter, a cautious and frightened child, who went down steps stepping twice – for safety – on the same step. I arrived never wanting to let my mother out of my sight. When she had to leave for work, I would cry. I arrived as Cubans would say *acomplejado*. That meant you were sensitive and ashamed, and puny and afraid, and harmless, and weak, and embarrassed completely all rolled up into one word. The word shares a relationship with the word complex which is the opposite of what a Cuban boy was expected to be. *Acomplejado* is possibly one of the worst things that could have been said about a Cuban boy who was expected to be simple, daring, and manly. *Acomplejado* was Piggy in William Golding's *Lord of the Flies* and it was me.

From the first day there my stepfather worked on changing that. Luckily, my stepfather had read Golding's novel and shared an affinity with Ralph and the boys who were essentially not Piggy. We played a game of lying in bed and throwing a tennis ball against the wall to catch it. He stood me on ledges to jump. He pushed me out of the house to run in the streets and hunt for lizards and bees. Hunting bees with a mason jar became my specialty. He took me to his job to meet his friends. He took me to swim in a make-shift decayed pool owned by two old British ladies who had been left in Cuba from before the Revolution and were straight out of the old Cary Grant movie *Arsenic and Old Lace*.

I was finally allowed to be outside during a downpour sliding down the street surfing on wet palm fronds. At my grandmother's house and under my mother's careful watch I was treated like a prized object which had to be protected. With my stepdad however, I became another boy whose knees were always scraped up and whose fear of personal demise began to disappear. I gained what every boy must have if he is to become a man. It is what adults would call the assured euphoric illusion of invulnerability. It means you think nothing *really* terrible could ever happen to you.

On Saturday mornings my mother and I would walk two blocks down Lawton and across Tejar Street to catch bus # 1 on its route back to my grandmother's house. The house where I lived before we moved in with my stepdad and his family. The house where I would find my grandmother sorting rice in the dining room and my grandfather sitting for lunch eating bread dipped in virgin oil with garlic and salt. My father asleep in his bed. While this was also not a nuclear family, it retained more order. My great-uncle Alberto sat on his bench listening to the news on an old

American radio from before the Revolution. Beba, my great-aunt, was in the small kitchen toward the back of the house. Iris, my cousin in her 20s, was chasing Beba around the house begging for one thing or another. Iris had a very high fever as a newborn which left her with the mind of a seven-year-old child. Yet, she could play the piano and write letters to our relatives in the United States. When I was a kid she loved me and played songs for me. We called her Iris, the Pianist. She also loved to answer the phone and would rush to be the one to pick up the one and only phone in my grandmother's house. Her letters to relatives were always a litany of names of people who sent greetings and people who were to be greeted, along with requests for vitamins, Vicks Vapor Rub, Alka-Seltzer, aspirin, and other items *"porque se necesita."* (because it was needed.)

Iris' father Ricardo always wore white and his bedroom was filled with food offerings to the many *orishas* (the spirit of a deity in the Yoruba religion) of his devotion; Ricardo practiced Cuban *Santería* and he was a priest in one of the orders that required him to wear all white every day. I used to sneak into his room to see the dusty old pots filled with coins and rotting fruit, the chains, and other random items I could not recognize which were offerings to his gods and saints.

Hands down, my grandmother was the matriarch of the house, though she was slim and petite. In fact, she must have weighed under 100 pounds at her heaviest. I called her *Tata.* When I slept over I would sleep in her room on a small cot next to my grandparents' bed. She would fan me to sleep when it was hot in the house. She would tell me stories. She was the first person I ever heard pray aloud. She taught me the Hail Mary and I would hear her repeat it, often wondering what this Mary in the prayer had that was so special that she could be more important than my grandmother. To me, that seemed an unlikely possibility. My grandmother embodied all that was holy and kind and worthwhile. I never once heard her scream, but I know she got her way around the house. I would often get mad at her and felt such shame afterward because I had screamed at a woman who never said anything back, other than Hail Marys.

One story that exemplifies my grandmother in my memory more than any other was when she took walks to visit a house about three blocks away from hers right off *La Calzada de 10 de Octubre*. She would take me with her. We'd stop in front of that house and she would say a prayer and then walk away. She did that for years. When I visited Cuba in 1996, I asked my grandmother if she still did that and we went and walked to that same house. She said a prayer and we walked away.

"Why do you go there every day you leave the house?"

"I made a promise a long time ago. A woman lived there and died there and she healed people. I came one time and asked for something and it came through. So I made a promise that if my prayer was answered I'd come here and pray and give thanks."

"What did you ask for long ago, *abuela*?"

"I can't remember anymore," she said.

Although she no longer had any idea of the prayer request that was answered, she still continued to be true to her promise. That was my grandmother: faithful, strong, stubborn, and true.

I now belonged to two very different and equally wonderful families. What was apparently at first the traumatic and terrible event of my mother divorcing and having to leave my grandmother's house was transformed into the experience that saved me from growing up sheltered and overprotected. At my step dad's (Tan) house I experienced people who argued and screamed and were loud and got mad at each other, often. I experienced being a normal boy who ran in the streets and chased other kids and played on the sidewalks and in the rain. I know my mother still feels terrible today for moving into the "relatives" house and not telling me the whole truth. I can't imagine now another way God could have found to make me a more real boy.

Last week when we were in Miami and Tan and I visited Mimi (his mother) in her nursing home, we found her sitting by her bed with her Depends adult diaper down at her knees. She could not dress herself. I cleaned her up and dressed her and threw away the soiled Depends and I thought of the pitiful little boy I was when I arrived at her Lawton house. I thanked God, and Tan, and my mother, and Mimi, for the man I had become.

MASTICATE AND SWALLOW

Even though I was chunky as a kid, I hated to eat. First off, in Cuba eating meant sitting in front of a plate of mashed *malanga*. Have you ever even heard of *malanga*? No. There is a reason. You've heard of potatoes, right? There is a reason. Potatoes taste good. *Malanga* is the ugly-tasting cousin. You mash it but it never looks right. It comes out gray. That is actually possible. Gray food. I ate gray food in Cuba.

Now imagine mashed *malanga* without butter and barely any salt. My mom would sit my cousin Sara and me down for lunch where she would have to shape the mashed *malanga* into the body of a man or a ship or an alien. Edible *malanga* sculptures. Anything to take our minds and taste buds away from the reality, the cold hard crushing truth, that because we lived in Cuba, and this was a communist country, where each family had a ration book, we would eat *malanga*. There is a reason you've never heard of ration books and trust me you want to keep it that way. The communist motto in Cuba was "Socialism or Death." More like, "Socialism or *Malanga*." Better: "Socialism is *malanga*."

My mother also had a motto: "Masticate and Swallow." She would stand over me, her commanding will ready to force the *malanga* down my windpipe if I resisted the other pathway beginning at my mouth. I hated to eat. "*Mastica y traga*." "Masticate and swallow". She didn't scream. She just repeated the slogan. I cried, but it never stopped her. She wanted me healthy and fat and full of *malanga* because the only other choice of a meal was sugar-water. Sugar water is tastier but far less nutritious than *malanga*.

Because *Malanga* was so disgusting, it also made me hate my cousin Sara. She would lie about eating her *malanga* and heap it on my plate while my eyes filled with tears.

"Mom, she put her mal-"

"Masticate and swallow!"

Sara did other mean things to me like placing a nail on my seat and pushing me around at school, and spitting water at me at restaurants. She'd call me "bed-wetter." She would make fun of me because I wore glasses and big shoes two sizes too big. I could overlook all that, but the *malanga* gifts were unforgivable.

You are wondering why my mom would use such a complicated word like "masticate" – couldn't she simply say "chew?" But in Spanish *masticar* **is** the word for chew. And masticate is *masticar*. My mom wasn't building my vocabulary, she was just imposing her will on her son. My mom was big on imposing her will. She had another motto which she enjoyed throwing around when I sobbed and ask the obvious:

"Why do I have to eat *malanga*? I hate *malanga*." Sob. Sob.

"Do you want to know why?" She asked. I'd fall for it. Walk right into it.

"Why?" I replied.

"Because, *aquí la que manda es menda*", she answered. That meant that here she was the boss. She was handing out the orders. I just had to follow the orders and eat the *malanga*.

So I lived out most of my childhood in Cuba being force fed. It wasn't just *malanga*. There was also forced *fabada* – a Spanish style white bean soup – it was liver, horse meat, Russian canned meat, and boiled *boniatos* (sweet potatoes). And above all, I had to like these foods because after my mother would order me to masticate and swallow, she also felt obligated to remind me that she made the rules saying, "After all, the food tastes good so I don't know what your problem is."

My cousin escaped my mother's food obsessions because my mother wasn't Sara's mother and could not very well impose her will on a child who was not hers. At the same time my mom swore that if she had it her way, "Sara would be eating *malanga* just like you. So would Fernandito and Israel and Griselita and the rest of the neighborhood kids. That girl is so skinny. If somebody doesn't do something soon, something will happen to her." Please God, don't let *malanga* happen to her. Anything else is fine: starvation, skin boils, firing squad, but not *malanga*.

My mother was not only obsessive about foods but also about medicines. For a period of what felt like 100 years she gave me daily *toques de garganta* (translated roughly as touches to the throat) which cured me of tonsillitis. The curing process involved wrapping her finger with thick gauze and covering it with iodine and reaching in and "touching" my throat. This was a daily gagging routine. She was obsessive about taking walks and going to churches to pray by touching the feet of the saints. She was obsessive about holding my hand in the street so I would not get run over. She obsessed with my schooling – I was the youngest kid in first grade at age five. I do have to admit that her obsessions were what got us visas to leave Cuba and move to New Jersey. Her persistence got us a visa out when everyone else in the neighborhood was left behind in Cuba drinking sugar water and eating *malanga.*

DANCE A BIT, MINGUITO

The great thing about Cuba in 1976 was that to be famous you did not have to be on television or be the guy throwing touchdown passes, you just had to be willing *to eat* glass. Minguito was one of the legends of my Lawton neighborhood in Havana. Old as dirt and wrinkled enough to prove it, Minguito shuffled onto Lawton Street once or twice a year.

And when he did, all children games would halt. Forget freeze tag, running bases, hide and seek, hopscotch – that was all nonsense. Forget holding hands in a hiding place with the neighbor's daughter while the other kids thought you were hiding or seeking. If you were a kid on Lawton Street in 1976 and Minguito shuffled in, the world stopped. We'd rush up to him begging, *"Minguito, baila un poquito."* Dance, Minguito, dance. And this heap of a man would shake, rattle, and roll.

But Minguito was best loved by us for eating glass. We'd search the block for shards as Minguito shuffled by. Kids flew up and down the block looking for a piece big enough so we could see it while it was masticated and swallowed down.

"Hurry."

"Find glass."

"Minguito is going to eat it."

The scene turned crazy. Pandemonium ensued as a dozen barefoot children feverishly ran around Minguito trying to slow him down, looking for glass. Would he eat a pebble? No. Throw that away. Keep looking. Divert Minguito's attention. Slow him down. You know what happens if he gets to the end of our block by Tejar Street.

While our moms would tell us to leave Minguito alone, we didn't listen. It was all fun and games until somebody got hurt and apparently Minguito could eat glass without getting hurt. So find that glass.

Now if he shuffled past our block you could never get him to eat glass. Never. He must have had another specialty for the kids in the next block. Maybe he juggled or played guitar. Where would he keep a guitar, though? More likely, he sang old *boleros,* the traditional Cuban love songs. I tried to imagine Minguito in his rags singing *"dos gardenias para ti."* (I have picked two gardenias for you.) No. He should stick to glass, I thought.

So we'd bring him a shard and Minguito would eat it. Oh, the glory. The sheer thrill of that moment when Minguito would stop and accept the glass in his dirty bloated hands. Then up to his mouth. We'd see it. No sleight of hand. He was not a homeless man trying to make a buck with a routine trick. He was really eating the glass. While it seemed like adults wanted to see him dance, we kids wanted him to eat glass so badly. After all, any man in Cuba could dance.

So who was Minguito? We did not know where he lived or where he was going. Did he have a family? Was glass eating something they all did? It didn't matter though, because when you are a kid, you don't need a lot of explanations, especially from an old guy willing to eat glass. And he did it with such joy. It's not every day a person willingly eats glass.

I remember the last time we saw him. He didn't want to talk to us. He was mad at someone or about something. We begged for dancing or glass eating. His face was darker, blacker than the usual shade of Minguito-brown. He looked confused. I remember stepping in front of him. Minguito looked past us and said something about doing something mean to our mothers. But typical Cuban insults about our mothers were not going to deter us from the glorious moment of seeing Minguito eat glass. So we pressed him and we pressed him. He got mad and pulled off his shirt to threaten us to fight. I still remember Minguito hopping around pitifully without a shirt, shaking his fists like this was his last line of defense against us. We ran home and watched him from the safety of our front steps. He didn't want to eat glass that day.

THE THREE KINGS

Not many people know that ancient kings traveled in airplanes. Luckily, *I am* one of those who know. Every January, from the front stoop of our Lawton Street house, my cousin Sara and I watched the early morning sky. Every year we'd see the plane bringing over the Three Kings a few days before January 6th when they were to leave presents in our house. They landed, every year, on *La Loma del Burro*, which translates roughly as the "hill of the donkey." The plane was massively wide and lily white. As I remember, the sunlight bounced off its whiteness giving it a hint of a silvery sheen.

"There it is! There it is," shouted my grandmother (Mimi) as we gleefully jumped up and down screaming for the three magical Kings. It turns out that historically those kings were neither magical nor royal. We knew of them traditionally for visiting the baby Jesus on the day celebrated as the Epiphany of Our Lord. They are named Melchior, Gaspar, and Balthazar, the wise men from the Orient who brought gifts to the baby Jesus by following a star.

In the Cuba of 1976, we did not question how it was that these Three Kings could come from Palestine, nor how they could possibly still be alive to deliver gifts some 2000 years later. No need to question that though, because the Three Kings – and we knew them by name – left us generous gifts each year. Gifts which our parents, in the communist imposed material poverty, could not manage. There was a lesson for us on the difference between material and spiritual poverty. We could fantasize about the Kings from Palestine, but communism was no fantasy. We knew, all the kids knew, that the government gave you the opportunity to buy three toys each year and that was in July. Your parents had to stand in a long line for two or three days sweating under the July sun. Of course, all the good toys were always gone by the time you got in the store. It was a communist imposed and manipulated Christmas in July. But the gifts of the Three Kings were lavish in comparison: a Zorro costume, a new desk with a mirror, and an assortment of toys the rest of the neighborhood kids could never believe. Don't get me wrong, we tried telling them where our gifts came from and that if they believed they could get gifts also. We tried and tried every year.

"You don't understand. Tell your parents to ask the three kings to come to your house!" All the other kids thought we were crazy to believe in these Three Kings. We were dismissed as delusional. But we got gifts every January 6th and they did not, and when you are seven you can't argue with that logic. The kings even left further proof of their yearly visit: half-eaten sandwiches, footprints; once we even found authentic camel dung in our front yard. Did I mention that the Kings flew over with their camels? That had to be true, for how else could they go up and down Burro Hill and deliver the gifts to our house. We knew that other kids in Cuba were also on the King's list, but we did not know any of those kids personally.

While I still do not understand the great lengths and self-imposed sacrifices our family had to go through to make that day possible each year, I do know that they prepared for months in advance, so that we could continue to believe. I don't know when you may stop believing in Santa Claus. And I hope that day never comes, though I know so much pushes you to not believe. You see, in Cuba, we just had so much less to believe in that could fill our world. To this day I have never stopped believing in the three magical Kings who came with their camels in planes all the way from ancient Palestine just to bring us gifts.

ON A SCHOOL FIELD TRIP

When I was in the third grade we all attended a small school near the Lawton Street house. In the mornings, my cousin Sara would walk with me to school. In school, we'd get a snack. Two small round cookies and a *malta*. There was no lunch. School gloriously ended at noon and we'd walk home to eat and to nap.

At school, we would have to wear the uniform of a Pioneer for the Revolution. The Communists were obsessed with brainwashing all of us to believe that if anything good happened it was only due to the Revolution. So, wearing red, white, and blue uniforms – the colors of the Cuban flag – was one way every child defended the Revolution from its enemies abroad and its traitors within. We were never told exactly who those enemies were other than being told "they were imperialist pigs."

In April, near the end of the year, we were told by our school's principal that our teacher was a traitor. The principal, a heavy-set middle-aged woman whose daughter was in my class, came to Room 3-A to tell us. "Your teacher is a worm. She is a counter-revolutionary. She has betrayed the homeland, *La Patria*." She closed with our pledge to the Revolution: "*Patria o Muerte. Venceremos.*" (The Homeland or Death! We will overcome!) Is this really how people talked? And about my teacher?

I went home and asked my stepdad what this meant. He had taught me how to jump off a ledge, how to catch a baseball, and how to tell if a woman was beautiful without even seeing her face, so I figured he had the answer. I stood in front of him as he pushed the chair back from his desk. He had been working on his movie notebook where he wrote about and rated every single movie he watched each year, when it was made, the director, the actors, and how many stars he'd given it. It was not a hobby, it was his religion, his act of worship.

"*Mira*". Look. I love that Cuban word. It covers so much ground. "Your principal hates people and she hates your teacher because your teacher is leaving the country and is not a communist".

Another of my favorite childhood phrases: "*se va del país*". This meant she was leaving Cuba. She was going to be free, wealthy, saved, she won the only lottery that existed in Cuba. She was going to the USA.

"Oh," I said

"Yes, your principal hates her because these miserable communists hate those who don't think like them and who don't approve every word Fidel Castro utters and says yes to everything that the government does."

"Oh," I said

"Remember last year when they arrested me for two days? Why did they do it?"

"Because you had long hair and you were talking to those two Italian tourists?" I answered.

"Yeah. Exactly," my stepdad said.

He told me not to worry, that one day we would also leave the communists behind. He said that we would go to the USA where people let you think what you wanted and didn't come ask you why you weren't doing community volunteer work or none of that nonsense. In the USA you could grow your hair long and listen to the Beatles loud on the radio and say whatever you wanted about anyone - not like in Cuba.

When I went back to school the next day we were told that we were going to do our duty as responsible citizens and friends of the Revolution, like the good little pioneers we were. We weren't just students in Cuba, we were Pioneers of the Revolution. Didn't we line up and promise every morning while we saluted that we would be like Che Guevara? Now we would have a chance to defend the revolution against one of its traitors. This is what Che would do against a traitor who sold herself to the Yankee Imperialists. Didn't we sing every morning that we were with Cuba, with Fidel, and with the flag against the enemy who always threatened her?

"Now we have our chance as little friends, as pioneers, of the Revolution." The principal ended her morning talk by telling us that the next day we would be taking a bus, a field trip to our teacher's house to do an Act of Repudiation to show our teacher she was an enemy of the people.

At home, that night my cousin Sara and I told my stepdad and our grandmother, my mother, and her great-aunt and anyone else who would listen. And we asked them what an Act of Repudiation was and what we needed to do.

"Tomorrow you won't go to school then," said my stepdad.

My mother replied, "He's going to school. He'll just stay in the back and won't join in when they sing the slogans against the teacher."

"Lourdes, how could you send him to school?" Questioned my stepfather.

"He has to go," my mother answered.

"Why?" He asked.

I watched and listened to the conversation all along rooting for my stepdad and mesmerized. I had never seen anyone stand up to my mother's will before that. It was always that she commanded and it came to pass. Command. Happen. What was he thinking? I was waiting for her to at any moment say to him, "Masticate and Swallow."

In the final argument, my step dad contended that it was wrong for me to go to school. Sara, as well as our grandmother and great-aunt Nenita were on his side. This only angered my mother who did not like to have her say questioned and especially when lots of people were watching.

"He is going to school tomorrow."

Thankfully, I was not asked to participate in the discussion because I would have had to side with my mother.

My step dad followed her around the house room to room and through hallways. He had the upper hand. His arguments made more sense. "Why should a boy from a family of worms go to an Act of Repudiation against his own teacher whom he loves? Give me a good reason," he said. Then he went near her to kiss her and I remember thinking he had convinced her. He was a master. When my mother turned to face him, I knew it was over even before she said the words, "He is going to school tomorrow because I am his mother and he is my son." Masticate and swallow that.

The next day I was at school early and Sara got to stay home. We walked the three blocks to my teacher's house and the whole school, not just the third grade, teachers and all, stood outside her house and screamed the slogans the government had taught us. For three hours of non-stop frenzy we pelted her windows with eggs and chanted: "Ping Pong, Out, Down with the Worm" and "Let her leave!" and "We don't need you!" Hours of the same mindless chanting of slogans. And though my plan was to stand in the back, I joined my classmates and chanted the slogans and spit at her house and threw the required eggs at her windows. We were dismissed right from her house after singing songs and hearing a speech from a man who thanked the Revolution and thanked Fidel Castro for giving him everything he had, even his dignity and his love for the good people of Cuba.

I walked home a dejected and angry child. But I did not understand the many difficult issues I had been asked to confront. I only knew that I had done all the things my family hated and that I had betrayed my teacher by telling her she was a worm. When I got home I lied and said I hid in the back. I took a nap and when I woke Sara tormented me by telling me she knew I had thrown eggs because Fernandito had seen me and he was proud because his family was a good revolutionary family. There was nothing I could say even though she followed me around the house taunting me saying that I was weak and a coward and a bed-wetter. My step dad told her to stop and that he never wanted to hear about that again. In my heart, I feared she was right.

THE COUSINS AND THE NEIGHBORHOOD KIDS

School would end for us right around midday and we'd walk home for lunch to an hour of *siesta*. Then we'd wake up to kid time. In Cuba, as I remember it, we never had homework which left us a lot of time to play in the neighborhood. My cousin Sara, my two younger cousins Titico and Edguita, and I would play outside every afternoon until it got dark. In the summers that was well past 8:30 PM giving us plenty of time outdoors.

We played all kinds of games that no longer exist or probably never existed until we made them up. We captured bees with mason jars and caught lizards to cut off their tails. We played hopscotch the Cuban Way. Sometimes my cousin Sara and other neighborhood girls would force us to play house. I was never good at that complex social game in which boys had to go out and work all day and girls stayed home with the baby. We'd bring back food from work, typically in the form of leaves and grass and hand that over to our wives who cooked and always collected our paychecks when we returned home. Each couple's house was typically one corner of the *portal* where we played. Arguments would flare up among "couples" because someone's "husband" did not bring enough "food" home or would not help with the kids. Then "wives" would visit each other's "homes" and you had to pretend to knock at make-believe doors and take the make-believe Cuban coffee you were offered when you visited. It was far too complicated for a nine-year-old boy like me.

My favorite game outside was to ride *la carriola*. I just have to draw it to explain it to you. Here is a picture of it:

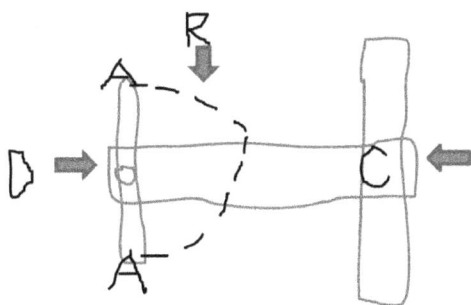

Some beautiful and amazing things cannot be described with words. You just have to see them. In this case, you also have to ride one. One long plank of wood crossed by two smaller planks. The front plank would swivel (D) back and forth for steering. Usually, we'd attach a rope (R) allowing you to steer from where you sat (C). And under it, the wheels (A) would be metal skates that we'd repurpose for the *carriola*. Lawton Street happened to go downhill, so you rode a *carriola* down and pulled it back up. Our moms would only let us ride it on the sidewalk, even though there were few cars in Cuba and fewer still on Lawton Street. If you say the word *carriola* to any boy of my generation, you will immediately make an emotional connection. It's like the "speak friend and enter" password to get into Moria from Tolkien's *Fellowship of the Ring*.

"Time to come inside!"

We feared and hated those words. They marked the end of the carefree joy and outside "kid time" and signaled baths and the combing of hair and the cutting of nails and having to eat *malanga* for dinner. In addition, nighttime also brought blackouts and roaches and my great-aunt Nenita, the hunchback, screaming at us and complaining to the other adults that we were running inside the house. She would always scream out the same line: "They are going to knock me down and crack my skull." It also meant school in the morning.

Jose Marti, the Abraham Lincoln Mark Twain George Washington of Cuba, said when he left Cuba to go to New York that *las palmas son novias que esperan*. The palm trees are girlfriends who wait for you. There could be other Cuban kids who left Cuba and are now old, like me, and think about the palm trees waiting for them back on the island. I doubt it, though. I have never once thought of a palm tree. I have wondered about my *carriola* on more than one occasion.

IT'S ALL FUN AND GAMES UNTIL SOMEONE EATS A DIE

Having to come inside was a punishment for us as kids. It only happened when it was raining really hard and with thunder or when it got dark. It rained a lot in Cuba, but even during rainstorms we were often allowed to play outside at my stepdad's house. When it got dark or if we were punished, or if there was too much thunder and lightning, we were stuck in the house. Being inside was usually a punishment. I would like to think that we liked being outside because we were healthy and strong and tanned and in top physical condition.

One day I asked Sara, "Why do we love being outside?"

"It's because we don't have AC in the house," she replied.

She made a solid point. When you are a kid, it's hard to want to be inside when your house is 900 degrees. Outside you'd feel the breeze under the shade. Maybe it would rain. You had multiple ways of cooling down. Inside, it was hopeless.

When we were inside at night we'd play a lot of *Parchisee*. I could explain it, but it would be just as easy for you to look it up online and get the idea. It's an old Indian game played in Spain and in the 1970's in Cuba. The thing about *Parchisee* is that to play, you need dice – two of them. Or at least one die which you are willing to roll twice, as needed.

Games of Parchisee at our house were epic battles pitting grandparent against grandkid and cousin against cousin; or typically, great-aunt Nenita, the hunchback, against all the kids. Arguments could take place. Things would get thrown about. It was a dangerous game, especially if you were winning. And as a kid, I loved winning. Sure. Playing was fun. It was a learning experience – and all that. Only one other person in the family loved winning more than me, my cousin Sara.

"You cheated again," my cousin Titico would tell her.

"Abuela!" Abuela!" She would wail.

Then we'd have to apologize to her for finding out she had cheated. In her logical universe, our role was to pretend not to see her cheat so that she could win, happily.

One night the game had gone on for hours with multiple cheating accusations having to be mediated by adults. Finally, at some late hour when we probably should have been asleep, the final piece in the game for my team, a yellow piece (I always chose yellow) was 3 spaces away from "home" and from a glorious win for me. My cousins watched hoping for Sara's demise. She hated to lose, but we loved to see her lose. So, there I was, with adults watching, ready to roll the die looking for a "3" and for a win.

Sara looked at me with the look of "listen, bedwetter, don't you dare roll a 3." I understood the look, but I rolled the die anyway. And it bounced and bounced and in slow motion I could see it – we all could – settling on a three. And right as the die was about to stop moving, something came out of what seemed to be the sky itself and plucked the die right from our eyes. The die vanished; it disappeared; evaporated. It was like the Assumption or like the Ascension. It was a mystical event. And my cousin Titico and Edguita and I stood up in awe. Aghast.

"How?" asked an astonished Titico.

"What did?" questioned Edguita.

"Did you?" I asked in an interrogating tone.

"I mean. I think. I don't" we all added sounds of disbelief. We struck the poses of the religious men in those famous paintings of the Apostles sitting around Jesus in marvel and in rigid unnatural poses. How could a die just vanish? And then slowly we looked at my cousin. She had it. She had the smile that the guilty wear. Sara was sitting there with a grin.

She stood and proudly proclaimed, "I ate it."

Rather than bearing a loss, she had taken the die in mid-roll and put it in her mouth and swallowed it. Now she could not lose, but neither could anyone else because we did not have another die. That was the last die we had and could not get another one on the spot. This is the part I will have to explain. You see, in Cuba, you could not just go to the local Walgreen's and buy some dice. It could be a whole year before we could get dice.

Next, I think there was screaming and tears. My stepdad came in the room and Nenita warned about some distant relative who had swallowed a die. Unfortunately, it had blocked her intestines and she had to have emergency surgery at Calixto Garcia Hospital in Havana. People in the room told her to shut up and to stop scaring the children. While I don't remember who it was, I remember the plan forming. The plan to retrieve the die.

"*Claro*. We will wait until you know, *you know*, it comes out the other side, and then we will know she is ok," my stepdad said. I don't remember how many days we waited, but I do remember playing *Parchisee* again a week or so later with a shiny and clean die that was not purchased, but retrieved.

LOSING THE ROOF AND THE FLYING ROACHES

One day, while I was in school generally being a good "Pioneer for the Revolution," our roof flew off. Lots of explaining to do here. First, you have to understand what it meant for a third or fourth grader to be a good Pioneer. Then I may have to explain the Revolution. Lastly, because of my deep respect for them, we'll deal with the flying roaches.

When I was in fourth grade I was a model Pioneer for the Revolution. I should probably capitalize that because, for Cuban Communists, there is no greater word than The Revolution. Being a Pioneer meant I behaved in school, always respected my teacher, the flag, Fidel, and the Revolution. It meant I showed up to school and read the National news in front of all the kids lined up in the school yard. The national news always told of the triumphs of the Revolution since back in 1959 when Fidel and the other revolutionaries overthrew Batista and marched into Havana riding on tanks while smoking cigars. Most of these triumphs were exaggerated or completely made up. We made more sugar; not just more, but record-breaking amounts; we completed the yearly production goals of vaccines for children; we helped the Angolan people free themselves from imperialist influences. Under Communism, the government only reported good news because under our "maximum leader Fidel Castro", and his family and a chosen exalted few who owned the country, bad news and bad things just could not happen. And if and when bad news or setbacks did happen, you could be sure that the Imperialist American Pigs were to blame. The imperialist pigs were the Yankees. Not the baseball team, but the American president, and the U.S. Congress, and the "rich fat cats" in those cartoons smoking cigars – in other words, the American government. A good pioneer always sang the songs of the Revolution condemning the Imperialists, the enemies of the Revolution, and the counterrevolutionaries, which is what they called any person who had different ideas than what the government taught. The best Pioneers were asked to stand guard during elections while the neighborhood people came to the CDR to cast their votes. The CDR on each block was the Committee for the Defense of the Revolution. We were always vigilant

31

and always defending the Revolution. In this way, the Communists made sure everyone watched and was suspicious of everyone else in Cuba and never ever potentially considered life in the United States as better.

Each block in each city or town had a house designated by the government as the CDR. The CDR people watched the block to make sure no one was planning to attack all the wonderful, but worthless, things the Revolution had given us. The Revolution claimed to have given all Cubans free education and free health care. Education meant brainwashing children; free health care for all meant no medicines available for most. This was certainly not reported because "only good things can happen in a Communist state." According to Communist logic, the Imperialist Pigs were always looking to find Cubans willing to want to overthrow the government. In school, we were taught to call these Cubans, "counterrevolutionaries." The CDR folks would make sure people were not meeting in a house to plan against the revolution. They were also responsible for approving folks who could go on ballots for elections. Of course, they only approved members of the Communist Party to go on a ballot to be elected.

My cousin Sara and I were asked one time to guard the voting urns during an election. We dressed in our Pioneer uniform - a white shirt with red shorts and a red handkerchief tied to the shirt. The irony is that the ballots people were casting only had candidates approved by the Communist government. Only one group could propose candidates and only one group of candidates were elected: members of the Cuban Communist Party.

I remember being so proud of guarding the vote and returning home to hear my stepdad say, "Don't be an idiot. You weren't guarding anything." "I was. I was guarding." I answered.

"You were guarding a lie," he retorted.

"I was helping the revolution," said I.

This is the part that was hard for a kid to understand. In school, we were always told that the Revolution was the most sacred thing we had. We knew that the heroes of the Revolution had triumphed. We knew that in 1959 Fidel, Camilo Cienfuegos, Che Guevara, and Raul Castro had given us the chance to be free from Yankee Imperialism. Now, at home, my parents were telling me we were Counterrevolutionaries. They told us very quietly because if the CDR folks overheard they could denounce us and my parents would have been arrested and jailed as Counterrevolutionaries.

After 1959 no one could drive a BMW or a Mercedes in Cuba because those cars were luxurious and belonged to Capitalists who "always took advantage of the working people." We were free of those people. Unless you worked for the government, we were also "free" of any cars. The logic in Cuba was that only some people having BMW's was unfair and unjust, so the fair thing to do was to have everyone *not* have a car. That was equality. That was justice. So, we all took buses and rode bikes and walked in 900-degree heat. After the Revolution of 1959 lots of things disappeared in Cuba: good cars, any car, Coca-Cola, bricks, roofing material, meat, Catholic priests, and bug spray for roaches, to name a few things.

The day our roof flew off my grandmother came to school to pick Sara and me up early.

"I need to get the kids. Our roof flew off," she said to the school secretary.

"That's fine. Sign here." The school secretary was not surprised. "Will they be in school tomorrow?"

The most abnormal things were common place in Cuba. When the roof flew off we still tried to sleep on the second floor, but the flying roaches came and landed in places I would rather not remember. They were dark brown and made a crunching sound when you stepped on them. The thing about flying Cuban roaches is that while they were walking on the floor or crawling on the wall by your bed, you could not tell if it was a *flying* roach. Not until you approached with the flip-flop ready to kill it, would the roach unfold wings and reveal its true persona. The wings coming out always struck a panic in us. It was like in *Fellowship of the Ring* when Gandalf is in Moria and he sees that the dark rumblings are not just Orcs. Oh no! It's a Balrog! A demon from the underworld! It was like when your mother picks up her *chancleta* (sandal or flip-fop) because she asked you to do something and you did not move. The flying roach has

33

the same capacity to cast a fear spell. In the mornings at school, I read all the glorious accomplishments of the Revolution. At night I fought off the flying roaches hiding under the sheets.

LENIN PARK

After we lost our roof in the Lawton Street house and on days when we did not have enough to eat, I'd stay at my grandmother's house. On the weekends, my grandfather would take me to Lenin Park where I could ride ponies and bumper cars. At one point, Lenin Park had a train, but I don't remember it ever running. I remember being walked around on a pony with my grandfather holding the reins and telling me that one day I would ride the horses outside the ring and without him holding the reins.

Lenin Park was just outside Havana. We'd ride the bus and then walk the rest of the way. I remember getting too tall for my favorite bumper car ride and my grandfather would show me how to bend my knees just enough to be shorter and be allowed on the ride when the man measured kids at the gate.

"If you ever fall out of a tree," (my grandfather would often start advice with a puzzling intro), "you want to make sure your legs bend when you land. Don't stiffen them, because that's how people break their legs when they fall off a tree. Keep them flexible." I wondered if there were a lot of Cubans falling off trees back when he was a kid? Could you not tell when you were going to suddenly need that skill?

"When you are in the dark all of a sudden," my grandfather began, "close your eyes. Count to ten. When you open them again, the dark won't seem as dark." I paid attention to this one since we had almost daily blackouts in Cuba because the government used rolling blackouts throughout the city in order to conserve power. This grandfatherly advice does actually work.

My grandfather also advised, "Don't scream at your grandmother. She loves you and wants to do what you want, but that's not always possible. Understand?" He was so kind and so soft-spoken; it was so easy for a kid to take advantage of that. My grandmother was so meek and so loving. I could take out my displaced anger on them. (The anger I could not direct at my father or mother.) And they never fought back.

My grandparents' house was built in the 1930s by my great-grandfather. The design was straightforward; one long hallway running down the middle from the front door with rooms to the left and right. The house was shared by the three Rodriguez sisters when I was a kid: my grandmother, my great-aunt Beba, and my great-aunt Chela. Their respective husbands also lived there, along with Iris, my cousin; she was the piano player. My father also lived there, but I always referred to the house as my grandmother's house.

When I slept over on weekends I'd wake up and walk to the back kitchen to sit on an old wooden bench that years earlier had been white.

"You should go back to bed. You are sleepy." My grandmother said that to me every morning.

"No," I'd say and ask her for water.

I used to ride a kid's tractor in the house's long hallway, pretending I was a bus driver on the #1 route which ran in front of my grandmother's house. Some nights, still, I dream I am on a bus route and it's always bus # 1 coming down *La Calzada de 10 de Octubre* passing El Café Colon, just after crossing the train tracks.

I still have vivid memories of my grandmother's house. My grandmother at the dining room table separating little rocks from a mound of white rice. My Tio Alberto hunched over his radio trying to listen to Cuban baseball games, Beba and Iris arguing about who would answer the phone. I can also remember my grandmother and two great-aunts sitting on the front porch on rocking chairs in the late afternoon, taking in the cooler breezes of our tropical island, talking about the day, the food they had cooked, about their husbands, and about all the people walking past the house.

I only remember two objects in my dad's room: a bed and a wardrobe. The bed was the one he set on fire one night when he fell asleep with a lit cigarette. He smoked when he was young. The wardrobe was full of graffiti that he himself had written on its inside doors. There were all kinds of quotes from writers I did not know then; one quote always caught my attention as a kid. It was something Gabriel Garcia Marquez had written about the poor remaining poor, but in Spanish, it is far more colorful.

My dad would spend hours inventing games for me to play. He invented a soccer game for me that used old baseball cards we had and a baseball game using dice. He taught me card games and number games and invented games using a pencil and a piece of paper. But it was always my grandfather who took me to Lenin Park to ride a pony or to go to the beach at Santa Maria, east of Havana. My dad's strength was thinking and my grandfather's was doing. I don't remember the two talking much to each other. My dad called my grandfather by his first name which was very strange because in Cuba where you always treat your parents with the informal "*tu*" and call them "*mami*" and "*papi*." The term "dad" can even have the variations of *pipo, papo, papito*. But it is never formal. Cuban culture curves deeply to the informal, even among strangers. In contrast, in Central American countries like Nicaragua and Costa Rica, children, even as adults, talk to the parents in the formal "*usted*." Maybe in those countries it would have been normal for my father to address my grandfather by his first name.

They did spend about a decade in the 1980's buying and selling flowers in the streets of Havana. They did not sell together, but they did gather in the mornings together with my grandmother to cut and prepare the flowers.

"Rogelio, *usted tiene flores que vender hoy?*" (Are you selling flowers today, Rogelio?)

I have always wondered what happened between them that created that distance. Did my father call my grandfather by his name as a kid? There are secrets in every generation that the old take to the grave. I used to think that all secrets were bad and that the truth had to be rooted out. Life has taught me that it is not truth, but kindness and love that must be rooted out, and expressed at all costs. Truth is secondary.

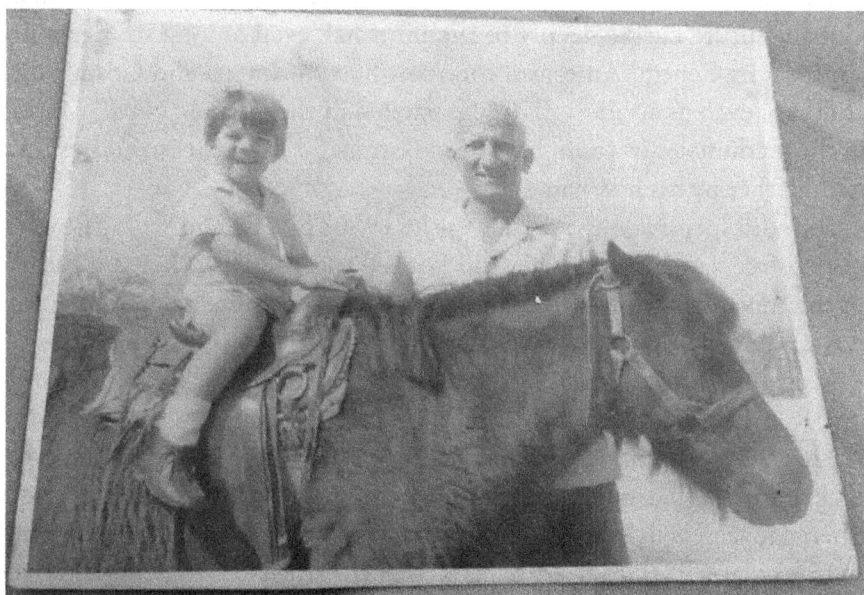

NAKED IN THE PARK

On July 4, 1976, when I was six, my dad went a little crazy over a woman who was not my mother. He ended up – we ended up – naked in the park. He was supposed to meet this woman at a restaurant and he had taken me along. Why, I'll never understand. You don't take your six-year-old to meet up with the other woman who you fell in love with on an old ferry ride to Casablanca across the bay from Havana. Evidently, because an old man sang you both songs from your past and you were both divorced and you thought she was magical. This was especially wrong since you knew she had dumped you for another man; I think the ex-husband. Either way, common sense tells you to leave your kid with his grandparents or take him to the beach or to the park or just about anywhere else. But my dad was a selfish and self-centered man who had no clue what to do with a six-year-old other than let him hang along like a buddy.

So we went to meet this woman. She never showed. Once he realized this, he walked off the restaurant line (in Cuba you had to wait in a line to eat in one of the few restaurants that were open) and went across the street to a park. Here we sat *criss-cross apple-sauce* on the ground, just like when he did when he was going to show me a new game. He undressed. Then he undressed me. And then we sat there. Naked. In the park. All I remember is being naked in the park. I'm not sure I even remember that. I do remember later that day sitting in a hospital or a police station crying. They had arrested him. I remember crying in a blanket until my mother showed up. I guess my dad thought he was Jesus so they kept him in a hospital for weeks and gave him electroshocks. They called that therapy. Afterward, he just came around and realized the Jesus gig had already been taken and decided he was not so perfect after all, even though I think he thought he had to be perfect for my grandfather. So there you have it.

I know this all happened on the 4th of July because years later he wrote a poem about the event. He published it in one of his books of collected poems. It does not even mention me being there. It mentions the woman and the ferry and the old man and the songs and the joy and the grief of being and not being with her.

Many years have passed since that day and I can go months or years without recalling it. For a long time I thought it was at the heart of my Cuban childhood – this traumatic experience. Then my dad visited from Cuba a few years ago and I had a chance to talk with him about that day. In hearing him describe it, I felt sorry for him rather than for myself. That was the day, the time in his life, when he was in his early 30s, and when he lost a woman he deeply loved. Perhaps, obsessively loved. But isn't most love obsessive? He has written her poems, love poems. He looked for her, and found her, when he visited Miami for the first time in the mid-1990's. It may have been all deeply wrong and it may never have worked out. She may have been the woman he had left my mother to pursue. And yes, all of that, objectively speaking, is messed up. But, humanly speaking about the life of my father, I now just feel terrible for him that day he lost his clothing and the love of his life.

And for me, now so many years later, this is just a bizarre story. It's not the heart of my childhood at all. It's not my grandfather or my grandmother, it's not Lenin Park; it's not hunting bees, or waking up the morning of January 6th after the Three Kings had been there. It's not even close to sitting by the sidewalk on the downhill as the rain waters crashed against me, or playing taco or wall ball with the tennis ball from "*La Yuma*." (This is the word Cubans in the 70's used to refer to the United States.) It's not my stepdad teaching me baseball and it's definitely not nights at my grandmother's house sleeping in her bed as we prayed a Hail Mary. And it's not the woman I always imagined as a child during that prayer when we recited "blessed are thou amongst women" and thought of my mom and my grandmother. It took me years to realize that sometimes you define yourself by this one bad experience that happened to you and over which you had no control and no fault. And then it took me more years to understand that you should never do that. Because in the end, that was not the big important thing my mind created it to be; it was not the heart of my childhood; it was also not the place that held all the mystery about what it meant to be a boy, or a son, or a grandson. It was just a weird day when as a six-year-old I was naked in a park.

LEAVING CUBA

Cubans have been trying to leave Cuba since 1959 when Fidel Castro and his Socialist and Communist friends took political power. The first wave of Cubans left right after the Revolution. They even sent their kids alone to the U.S. through Operation Peter Pan with the help of the Cuban Catholic Church. Parents were trying to spare their kids from the violence of the Revolution. Then there were those who left when Castro nationalized companies. That meant he stole companies from private owners and those became property of the Revolutionary Government. Then there was the Cubans who left through Camarioca in 1965 and the Freedom Flights until 1973. But the big exodus came in 1980. In 1980 there was the Mariel Boatlift. My family did not get to be lifted by a boat and I'll explain why. Actually, first was the Peruvian Embassy. Then the boatlift. Then, eight months or so later there was a flight from Havana to San Jose, Costa Rica on Iberia, the national airline of Spain. For me, this airline is the international symbol of freedom and escape and hope and new opportunity all in one.

First, I should explain that leaving Cuba is a national obsession. Cubans have tried to leave in rafts and makeshift boats and why they have been willing to go to just about any country that is not Cuba. I still have dreams where I am stuck in Cuba and I have missed the flight to leave. It's not at all that you think you have to go to the U.S. because there the streets are paved with gold, that the sidewalks are gold, that your dog and your cat eat in gold food bowls. Communists will tell you it's about the money and that those of us who wanted to leave were selfish and greedy and that we did not care for the common good. They called us who left "scum" and "worms." It was not long after we left that I understood the lies behind the promises and the slogans of Communism.

I mean, we did think the dogs in *La Yuma* ate from gold bowls as kids, but that is not at all why Lourdes and Jorge –let's call my mom and stepdad by their names for this story – wanted to get out. It's because Lourdes wanted to be a lawyer, but the government did not allow people who were not loyal Communists to pursue a career in law. It was because Jorge wanted to listen to the Beatles and have long hair and not worry about doing volunteer hours in his neighborhood watching for an imperialist invasion that was a complete fabrication. It was because Lourdes did not want her ten-year-old son to be sent to do school outside of Havana for months at a time and be forced to work on an "education farm" without his family. This tactic was used by the government to isolate children and teach them the "truths" of the Revolution. Jorge wanted to be able to buy a car one day or read a newspaper that was not published by the government. He wanted to be free of constantly being watched by the local CDR goons. He wanted to grow his hair long and speak with foreigners in Italian or French.

Families wanted to leave Cuba so badly that one day in 1980 a bunch of men crashed a bus through the gates of the Peruvian Embassy in Havana. As a result, hundreds, thousands of Cubans flocked in to seek asylum. They were begging the Peruvian government to get them out of Cuba. There are a few good books about this and you should read them because it is part of history. If those men I didn't know had not crashed a bus through those embassy gates, I'd still be in Cuba. I also discovered that two years earlier two other men had attempted the same idea by climbing the wall into the embassy, but no one else followed. The Cuban government jailed them. One of those two men is Esteban Luis Cardenas, a close friend of my father. I visited Esteban Luis in a retirement home in Miami years later. Esteban was in a wheel chair and had trouble speaking then, from the beatings he had received in prison from the government who did not want him climbing over walls into embassies.

The day of the Peruvian Embassy invasion, I was with my dad and my mom could not get a hold of him. We were somewhere in Old Havana walking to meet a friend of his and we walked right into the crowds running to and away from the Peruvian Embassy. The streets were blocked. My dad and I were caught in a group moving in all directions, away from police trying to control the scene, then towards a group of Communist government sympathizers screaming "Scum! Let them leave! Scum," while they threw garbage at us. I was just a ten-year-old kid, but I remember wondering what we were doing there.

A couple of months later President Carter allowed Cubans in the U.S. to sail boats to Cuba to pick up family members the Cuban government allowed to leave. This was called the Mariel boatlift because the boats from the U.S. were only allowed to dock at the port of Mariel just west of Havana. A family meeting about the Mariel Boatlift took place in the large family room one afternoon at Tan's house on Lawton Street. Family members gathered from my mother's side of the family and from Tan's side. The issue was that a boat had come from Miami, but only three family members would be allowed by the Cuban government to go back on the boat. The families now had to choose the three. The discussion lasted well into the night and many different people were considered to potentially leave.

"Send Fabio," someone suggested at one point.

The prospect of me leaving Cuba without my mom and without my stepdad became a possibility, but never happened. After a lot of loud conversations and some disagreements, my maternal grandfather (Alberto Martinez Herrera), my stepdad, and a distant nephew were the chosen three. A few weeks later the three men left Cuba on a boat. They left out of Mariel and were at sea a day and a half before arriving at Miami. The rest of us were left behind.

For about six months we thought we were left behind permanently and that was a really scary feeling. My mother managed a visa to Costa Rica for both of us. In September of 1980, we flew on an Iberia jet from Jose Marti International Airport just outside Havana to San Jose, Costa Rica. I remember smelling everything on the plane - the napkins, the seats, the magazines. I had never seen or smelled so many new things. Years later, I don't remember anything about the plane, but I do remember getting to the airport early in the morning at a time when the world was still quiet enough and just waking up. I remember being behind a hard glass wall inside the terminal and seeing my father outside. I did not know that I would not see him for sixteen years, but I knew that he looked still and quiet outside with his arms at his side, helpless, not wanting to move, forcing a smile on his face.

At the beginning, I mentioned that there were things I lost in Cuba. My grandmother, my grandfather, my father, and all of my family on that side were the things I lost. All the people I have talked about in these stories about my childhood in Havana. But I also said that the hand of God played a part in this story, so no matter how sad this sounds now at this point, as I am leaving Cuba, I promise you that God will make sense of it later. A lot of stories in life will be that way. It won't make sense as it happens and as it hurts you and rips your heart. But, if you wait, if you just hang in there and trust, then the story unfolds and you see your part in it you realize there was a bigger scene that was working out through you. And there were chances to love and be loved. And for me, that was Elizabeth, New Jersey.

Part II: Elizabeth

LA CUBANA

When we first moved to Elizabeth, New Jersey in 1981, it was after living in Miami for three months, and that was after living in Costa Rica for three months. We left Cuba on an Iberia flight. We left Miami on a bus. The bus was not a Greyhound. We were Cuban and Cubans traveled in "La Cubana" which moved Cubans from Miami to New York, daily. The Cuban Greyhound arrived in Elizabeth at the bus depot which doubled as a restaurant on Elizabeth Avenue: "*El Pimiento Rojo.*" The Red Pepper, one of three Cuban restaurants on Elizabeth Avenue in the 1980's. The other two were "Alvarez Café" and "El Palmar." El Palmar is where Tan, my stepdad, would work a year later delivering *cantinas*, restaurant cooked meals delivered daily to your house. "El Palmar" is where I would have my first summer job as his cantina delivery helper.

In the beginning, Elizabeth seemed small and all the buildings crowded together brown and gray. My grandfather referred to Elizabeth as "*Guanabacoa*" which is a small country town east of Havana. He waited for me and his daughter, my mom, at "El Pimiento Rojo" when we finally got off the twenty-hour trip on the Cuban Greyhound. This was it. Now we had really arrived in the USA. This is the place my parents told me about in Cuba: New York City, the center of the universe. *La Yuma. La USA.*

I had all kinds of warped expectations about the USA. This was the place where every kid owned a car, and the sidewalk walked for you, and where the cat's food bowl was made of gold. This was the place where you did not have to go to work or school and if you did, your servants carried you there. Miami had been a pit stop, a limbo, a purgatory between the two extremes. Moses could not have been happier crossing the Red Sea. And Elizabeth delivered.

Everything was better. Miami was Cuba. This was *La USA*. It was cold. The people *looked* American. The buildings looked old and mysterious. It snowed flurries on our second day. We lived in an attic; I had never even heard of an attic and now I lived in one. Radio WADO (pronounced Wah-Do), a New York radio station, played Bustelo Cuban coffee commercials all morning long as my grandfather woke me up to go to school. In the mornings, it seemed like every five minutes I heard the jingle:

Bustelo es un señor café
Un café con clase
Bustelo es mi café.

Bustelo is an awesome coffee
Bustelo is a coffee with class
Bustelo is my coffee.

I listened to Malin Falu and Fabian Caraballo y Baez on WADO on 1140 AM while my grandfather rubbed my back to wake me up. Yeah, this was our city. This was our café. These were our snow flurries, our USA. We did not have maids to carry us from room to room, but so what. I had the Mrs. PacMan video game at the Laundromat, baseball cards with the pink gum inside, and friends who played and taught me to play football. I had never before seen a sports ball that wasn't round. I had friends who spoke in a language I started slowly to understand: the language of "Atari" and "Risk," the game of world domination. I had *Little House on the Prairie* and *Happy Days* on TV every afternoon. I had *M*A*S*H** and *The Honeymooners* late at night.

I could not own my own "Atari" or "Risk" at first, too costly for our attic lifestyle. But one day I found a used "Risk" game in a garage sale and bought it for five bucks. And some years later when "Atari" was replaced by "Atari 7600," I saved up money from a summer job and bought the old model. I was old school before old school was cool. I had "Risk." I had garage sales. I had a grandfather who smoked a pipe and drank too much only on weekends and had violent coughing fits that woke me up at night to see him in his "C.H. Martin's" long one-size too big thermal underwear.

I had train trips to Princeton with my grandfather and occasionally we rode into the city (New York City) on the NJ Transit trains. We walked everywhere. Once in the middle of a January cold spell my grandfather and I walked home from the Elizabeth train station to Orchard Street. We arrived with our boogers frozen on our upper lips and with thighs near frostbite. My mom managed to get her first job in Elizabeth at a Dunkin' Donuts even without a car. My grandfather got paid for taking English classes he was never interested in taking. I had my walk home from sixth grade sliding over ice- so many memories of our beginnings in "*La Yuma*."

Waking up, I'd ask my grandfather. "How cold is it today?"

"Sixteen. Fahrenheit." He answered.

I had Fahrenheit. In Cuba we only had Celsius. And I had Radio WADO:

Bustelo el número uno
De nuestra comunidad
Bustelo el que más se toma
Por algo será verdad.

Bustelo the number one
Of our community
Bustelo the one everyone drinks
That's why we are telling the truth

I had Mrs. Stoner, our sixth-grade teacher, showing me how to say cowboy instead of "koh-boy." But the main thing I remember about that first year in school was pumpkin carving in late October. On Halloween, I wore my dad's clothes and painted red lipstick on my face to create an instant costume: a bleeding madman. When we got to Christmas, I had a little plastic tree and lots of Star Wars toys and action figures. These were gifts that were out of proportion with our attic budget. While I did not have a new Commodore-64 with a disk drive like my friend Rich, I had more. He did not know about La Cubana, Celsius in Cuba, Bustelo coffee, Radio WADO, pink gum, the newness of snow, *la Yuma*, koh-boy, and the ESL class with Mrs. Stoner. He was born in Elizabeth at zero. I was born in Elizabeth at ten. You appreciate it so much more when you are ten years late, but not too late.

ORCHARD STREET BASEMENT

When we first lived in Elizabeth, we lived in a basement without heat for an entire winter when weeks went by and the temperature would not rise above 32 degrees. This basement was on 51 Orchard Street in a house owned by a Portuguese husband and wife. The husband loved Volkswagen Rabbits and had a huge black dog in his backyard along with lots of Portuguese wines in big-bottomed bottles with long skinny necks. They lived on the first floor, rented the second, the attic, and the basement. The attic had rooms for boarders at a person per room, sometimes a couple, for $30-40 dollars a week. When my mother convinced my stepdad to join us from Miami all three of us lived in one room in the attic and shared one bathroom with all the other boarders.

But the basement was no way "renter's ready." In fact, a part of it was used for storage: boxes, old clothes, vinyl records, construction and lawn tools, broken electronics, and a pool table with other pieces of furniture stacked on top of it. This left us a small living room, a kitchen, a tiny bathroom, and one bedroom. While the basement was unheated, we did have one source of heat - an electric heater we kept in the bedroom along with our coats, which we'd have to wear in order to go to the bathroom or the kitchen at night.

When Heberto Padilla, the Cuban poet who lived in Princeton with his wife and son, visited us he sat in the living room with his coat on and with my grandfather who rented an attic room in the same boarding home. To commemorate Padilla's visit, my stepdad cooked his famous "*tortilla española*" with *chorizo* in the kitchen, wearing his long black coat and a scarf.

After a few rounds of drinks, Padilla would end up saying, "*Este hogarcito esta esplendido,*" referring to our basement, which he found to be splendid. Of course, he didn't have to sleep there sharing a bedroom with his parents, wearing a coat to go to the bathroom, wondering if the electric heater would tip over at night sending the place up in flames. No, Padilla saw the place through his thick glasses with the eyes of a man who had drunk too much, but I didn't need alcohol to feel that it was indeed fantastic.

In many ways, Elizabeth was my first love in America. I adored Orchard Street. In fact, the houses and the people there became the model of the quaint American town. I'll never forget the smell of that first Fall, a mixture of camping and home. I loved the leaves raining down as I walked home from Alexander Hamilton Middle School.

In winter, I loved the cold and the snow. I loved bundling up with scarf and gloves and a coat to go out - it felt adventurous. I felt protected with all the layers. It seemed that if someone had tried to mug me they would need a twenty-inch knife just to leave a scrape. I even loved the strange language I heard coming out of windows and out of cars as they drove by. All of this became for me a confirmation that I had more secrets to learn about this American town. I loved Elizabeth.

PATHMARK AND HAM

When we lived on Orchard Street and the winters were unbearable, and the snow piled on our basement door so that we had to push and push our way out, my stepfather had to steal food from Pathmark. Usually, it was ham. Why ham? It is thinly sliced and comes in a package that resembles a book: rectangular. It fits well in a briefcase. He and I would walk into Pathmark on nights when he only had a dollar or two - in change. We'd walk up and down the aisles, my stepdad with his briefcase, dressed in his shirt and tie, just home from teaching an Italian, French, or Spanish class at the Berlitz School in Summit, New Jersey. He would have to hitch rides or catch a collection of buses just to teach for a couple of hours at seven bucks an hour. Because he only got part-time work, a handful of classes, he'd go for weeks without a big paycheck.

So we'd walk into Pathmark and he'd be telling me to watch one way while he stuck ham in his briefcase, and some cheese every once in a while. Sometimes his briefcase was too full and he'd stick the ham down his pants. Holding it with his belt and pulling his shirt out to cover it. Some days it would be ham in the pants, eggs in the briefcase, bacon here, lettuce there. "The eggs for *la tortilla Española*," he'd remember. "Throw a red pepper in there. We need that too."

"Stop dad. You are getting greedy now," I scolded.

"Just watch for me. Did that man see me?" He asked.

"No, dad," I promised.

"Check. Look at me. How does my shirt look?" he'd say, sucking in his gut. "Can you tell?"

"No, dad. I can't tell you have ham in your pants," I assured.

"Where's the ketchup?" He added.

Out, we'd walk, only paying for a dollar loaf of sliced bread while my dad carried about twenty-five dollars more worth of food than what we had when we came into Pathmark. On the walk home we'd hide behind a building and he would "unfood" – out the ham! Out eggs! Out lettuce! On Prancer and Dancer and Dasher, Santa is bringing food home tonight. Out green pepper and red! He would be happy thinking about the tortilla he would make, and about having a ham and cheese sandwich for lunch the next day.

"I forgot *chorizo*!" He exclaimed, remembering. "No, dad! No. Let's keep walking home. We don't need *chorizo*." "But a tortilla with *chorizo* would be something," he concluded.

On the way home, we'd pass the corner liquor store, where on a special occasion he had once bought a bottle of *Amaretto Di Saronno*. We'd also pass the open corner lot where I made my first snow man at the age of ten. He was puny, but I loved snow. My mother hated when he stole from Pathmark. I did not mind it so much; We struggled to live without heat in the winter, living without food would have been impossible.

I was with him the day he finally got caught shoplifting at Pathmark. A few men grabbed him and stuck him in a small room with lots of small television screens by the entrance of the store. He pretended he did not know me, that I was not with him, that he was a distant uncle. I called him by what all my cousins called him when I arrived at the Lawton Street house years earlier, Tan, so the men who were holding him could not tell if I was his son. But no matter what I called him, he had been my dad for many years by the time we were in Elizabeth.

One of the big guys told me to go home. I waited outside the door of the small room waiting for him to get out. Panicked, I wondered how I would break the news to my mother. I imagined him being taken away in handcuffs. I imagined having to be without him while he was in jail. No heat. No food. No dad.

He came out of the room a few minutes later and we just walked out. Nothing else. He told me they scared him and told him he could never come back to Pathmark, a lifetime ban. Years later, my friend Rich and I chased a man who had mugged a woman in the Dunkin' Donuts parking lot into that same Pathmark. It had been years since I had been in there. The manager closed all the exits. They caught the man. Some big guy thanked us and we went home.

PINTO CATCH-22

Once we moved to Elizabeth Avenue my parents were able to afford to buy Heberto Padilla's 1970's Ford Pinto station wagon. Of course, the car was a death trap, but they had only paid Padilla $300 dollars for it. It was brown. It had no heat for the winter and no AC for the humid Jersey summers. The driver's door was rusting off, the odometer was frozen, and the radio only picked up AM stations; we could listen to NY Mets games on it, but that's about it. When it rained or snowed the windows had to be kept up and the front windshield would fog up.

"Don't touch it with your hand," my dad, Tan, would scream.

My father had this theory about putting grease marks on the windshield if you touched and wiped it with your hand.

"*Búscame un trapito.*" He'd ask for a rag. From the back of the station wagon would come a dirty sock or a used Dunkin' Donuts napkin.

"Wipe your side! *No veo nada.*" (I can't see anything.) He'd lower the window to wipe his mirror, while the snow, the sleet, the rain, came flying into the Pinto. One time the key holes on the doors froze and my dad spent thirty minutes cursing at the Pinto in the cold.

"*Carro de porquería.*" (Lousy car! You are worthless!) He yelled at the Pinto.

"Don't say that," my mother piped in. "The car has ears; it has feelings; it can hear you." Just like our dog and our television – all had feelings according to my mom. The dog would leave poop all over the hallway of our apartment. My dad would walk to the bathroom sleepily at 11 AM. He worked the night shift as a security guard full-time now. He would step in it or dance to avoid it and wack himself on the homemade bookshelves made of gray bricks and planks of varnished wood.

"*Perra de porquería.*" (Lousy Dog! You are worthless!)

"Don't talk like that to Katia. She understands what you said." My mother admonished. The TV understood too when it lost reception or the *cambia cambia* (the clicker) would not work.

"*¡Ay, Qué suerte la mía!*" (Just my luck!) My dad was always a tad on the melodramatic. He drowns in a glass of water, my mother would say. I think I inherited that or learned it and I'm still trying to work through it.

The Pinto was great. It took me to school. It took my dad to his security guard job. It took us to Foodtown, by now he no longer needed to shop with a briefcase. It even took us to New York City on good and rare occasions. Only one problem with the Pinto and it wasn't the Pinto's fault, but rather a gross injustice of the entire Elizabeth Police Department. The problem was parking tickets.

My dad worked nights and parked days. And we lived on a busy street in downtown Elizabeth, a street with parking meters. You had to feed the meters quarters from 8 AM to 6 PM and my dad slept from 8-3 PM. Our day, his night. This worked fine as far as him getting the rest he needed. The house was quiet with me in school and my mom at work. This wasn't good for parking, however. On a bad day, he'd get three or four tickets. On a good day, he'd get away with one. The glove compartment in the Pinto was full after his third month on the job. Most tickets faded in the sun, some of them were wet from the rain then dried in the heat of the glove compartment where they faded out of recognition. My dad was a collector. Hundreds of tickets. Eventually they exploded out of the glove compartment and into the wagon's trunk with old newspapers, sneakers, *trapitos*, and ants.

"Dad, why do you keep them?" I asked.

"Can't pay them. Eight dollars a ticket, sixteen dollars after a month when you are late. Can you imagine? I'd live to pay tickets! Get up. Feed the meter. Every two hours. What kind of sleep would I get? I'd have to sleep two hours, run downstairs in my old red shorts with holes, put quarters in the meter. What if I don't have quarters? Go down the street to the Greek lunch counter for some change. 'Oh, my friend,' the Greek will say to me. 'I take care of my customers first, my friend in the red shorts with holes and little sleep.' After that, it's wait for the Greek. Wait for the Greek. Feed the meter. Run upstairs. Shut up Katia. *She has feelings.* Sleep. Do it all again in two hours. *Me vuelvo loco.* (I'll go crazy.) The heck with the tickets!"

And with that long statement of faith, my father became the most wanted parking offender in the history of modern parking meter enforcement.

Thankfully, they never towed the Pinto. They just kept writing tickets. Poor Pinto, it wasn't his fault. He was just parked there.

So if my dad got rid of the Pinto, no more tickets, but no more full-time job. If he kept the Pinto and fed the meter, no more sleep, so no more job. If he kept getting tickets and paid them, no more money, so why the job. My father reasoned if he kept getting tickets, who gives a heck. "I'll keep collecting!"

"How many did you get today dad?" I asked, almost afraid of the answer.

"Two. Slow day," he'd say.

When he changed jobs to work nights at the airport driving the courtesy van for guests, he'd bring home chocolate croissants, tips from the van passengers, and more parking tickets.

ALEXANDER HAMILTON

When I was in seventh grade I walked to Alexander Hamilton Middle School. Some mornings I'd stop at the Greek restaurant where, for 35 cents, I could get butter and jelly on white toast. I would walk up Elizabeth Avenue toward Broad Street passing the Elizabeth Public Library on my left, where years later with Rich and Ken I would steal books by throwing them out the window. On my right was the Elizabeth Courthouse where, also years later, I would sit with Laura K under the concrete lions and fall in love. But all that was much later. As an eleven-year-old I walked under the railroad bridge where the water would freeze into stalactites in the winter. I'd hang a right at the Elks Club, where I went to my first high school dance, and cross Murray Street, where Isabel G lived. I'd walk past the funeral home, where we knew they put dead bodies in natural poses to make it look like they were alive so the family would not worry about them so much. Some of them they sat right in the front parlor of the funeral home and you could see them through the window. They'd do that so that if you really missed them, you could drive by and wave and say "hi."

I'd walk past the tall brown building where all the old people would walk past me with their metal carts. One more block and I'd cross West Jersey Street and the building for the Girls Scout Council. Then came the climb uphill to the railroad bridge, the old overpass of a now abandoned train track which ran through the center of Elizabeth. And then one short downhill block to Alexander Hamilton Middle.

I ate a free breakfast and a free lunch at Hamilton. When I got to school early, I could get a small carton of milk and a plain greasy donut. They call these "old-fashioned donuts" now because that's much easier to sell than if you were calling them old plain greasy donuts. I loved this school. The first time I saw it snowing, the first real snow fall I saw, was out of the window of my English as a Second Language (ESL) class on the second floor. Class stopped so that all these kids from Cuba, Philippines, Honduras, and a bunch of other tropical third-world countries, could gawk out the window and marvel and ask the American child question: "Will there be school tomorrow?" We looked at our teacher and waited.

"Oh, you children, already so Americanized," responded Ms. Stoner.

I didn't even know what homework was until I was at Alexander Hamilton Middle School. It was, in fact, the first Secretary of the Treasury of the United States who introduced me to homework. Alexander Hamilton first went to school in the U.S. in New Jersey, just like me. We had quite a bit in common. I can imagine back in the 1770s when he was first introduced to homework it was probably quite a shock to him since he was coming from the West Indies. Something else we had in common: both came to the U.S. from an island in the Caribbean. So basically, he wasn't Cuban, but he could have been.

"Son. May I call you son?" Alexander would have started in a deep voice.

"Why, yes, Mr. Hamilton. Call me son."

"Well. There is work you do in class, you see. Then there is work you do at home. That's homework."

"I see. But if I don't do it at home? Is it then classwork? Because I am very busy at home watching *Little House on the Prairie* and *Happy Days* and playing *Risk* and football with my friends who speak English, like you."

"Son. Homework builds character. It helped me become Secretary of the Treasury."

"Yes. That's important. And being shot and killed helped you become the reason my school is named after you."

"Exactly."

I think that's how that conversation with Alexander Hamilton would have happened, but I did not speak much English in the sixth grade when I arrived at the school in Elizabeth, New Jersey, and the homework reality hit me.

I also tried learning the tuba at Alexander Hamilton. I could have picked a cooler instrument like the drums or at least one easier to carry. You didn't see cool guys carrying tubas; they had the saxophones, clarinets, and drumsticks. It was the only instrument available, unfortunately. I took a total of three lessons and quit the tuba. It was just too heavy.

At Alexander Hamilton, I had friends with last names like Kandl, Clayton, Magnussen and Duzeminski, and teachers with names like Bufalaski, Stoner, Moffet, and Boguyevski. I shared a locker with Raymond M, the shortest and meanest kid in class. I am sure he rode a Harley and by the seventh grade had the tattoos to prove it. I was the second shortest kid and he was the shortest. But something about his face and his name clearly told you that messing with him would end you up in the nurse's office on the second floor. He would let you know you were a moron no matter how tall you towered over him. He had long hair and had a jean jacket with the sleeves cut off. Did he smoke? I think he smoked.

In seventh grade, Arnold K introduced me to "Dungeons & Dragons" and taught me the words to the song played at the beginning of every M*A*S*H* episode. How did it go?

Through early morning fog I see
visions of the things to be
the pains that are withheld for me
I realize and I can see

that suicide is painless
it brings on many changes
And I can take or leave it if I please

The game of life is hard to play
I'm gonna lose it anyway
The losing card I'll someday lay
and this is all I have to say

I don't know if that's right but if you hum it you'll see it makes some sense anyhow.

It was in seventh grade when I fell in love with every girl in my class, but especially Lucy O. Her name just sounded like it came right out of a Beatles song. She cheated off me in math a couple of times and that was the extent of our relationship. I am sure if you were to find her today she's more likely to remember a bug than the kid she copied off in math class. But I remember.

I remember Nancy D. winning every award, every year, along with Carole something or other who was skinny and pale. I remember being sent to the auditorium when a teacher was absent and they would not hire a sub. Mr. Matchacara, the principal, was short and tough and mean – like Raymond Magnussen, who is probably a principal today. He'd look at you and you stopped talking and moving and feeling. I remember my 8th-grade English teacher who sat at her desk all year and made us read *Lilies of the Field* and *Anne Frank*. I thought that middle school English class was an attempt to turn the Raymonds of this world into stuffy English professors.. I remember making "Beef Stroganoff" in Home Economics class and learning how to sew. We also had "Mechanical Drawing" and "Wood Shop," where I think I managed to make one or two abstract useless objects of wood while others made elaborate bird houses.

I remember 8th grade graduation having just turned thirteen, singing "We are on top. We know where we are going. Way on top. We are sure that it's showing. And we just feel like shouting hurray, shouting hurray." Even at thirteen, I was still a child. I was a child and Alexander Hamilton Middle School was my childhood.

A TYPICAL DAY ON ELIZABETH AVENUE

When Rich and Ken were twelve and I was a year older, we'd go to the Main Branch of the Elizabeth Public Library every afternoon after school. Rich would get his parents to drop him off at my apartment and Ken would walk about fifteen blocks. The library was at the corner of Broad Street and Elizabeth Avenue. I lived two blocks away, past the Carvel Ice Cream Shop, the Greek lunch counter, and the cigar shop. There was also a Salvation Army Church across the street with its band playing every Sunday morning around 7 AM. Those two blocks were littered with memories for us. The downstairs hallway of the building where I lived where Rich and I once found a homeless man sleeping next to the gas heater. The alley next to Kolker's toy store where Rich did roundhouse kicks practicing his few lessons in Tae Kwon Do. The other alley where my grandfather once forbid me to bring home a kitten that I wanted to rescue which was covered in fleas. The front of the library where Ken threw Rich's new sneakers in the middle of the street for the fun of it.

Sometimes Ken hitched a ride with Rich's parents, but mostly he walked or rode his Schwinn "Stingray" bike with the banana seat. Then they would stand in the street and yell up at my third-floor window facing Elizabeth Avenue. We did not have a door bell. My building was three floors. My dog Katia would bark and I'd throw the keys down so they could open the door and come up.

We'd walk to the library, go in, and head for the Young Adult (YA) section where they kept a "Vote for your Favorite Book" box. By looking at the votes in the box when no librarians were watching, we found out that *A Wrinkle in Time* was in the lead. Trying to be funny each afternoon we would vote and vote often on behalf of our choices for best YA book: *A Wrinkle in my Face, A Wrinkle and a Twinkle, A Wrinkle on My Nose, A Wrinkle? No! Plastic Surgery*. We put in so many votes That we were honestly disappointed when none of our choices of fictional work of fiction would pull into first place week after week. Surely there was fraud involved.

Promptly after exercising our American right to vote, we'd go look for books or sneak into the little elevator reserved for staff. We once rode down to the basement, the area the sign on the stairs warned: "Reserved for Staff". We were disappointed to find more books in the basement. No secret potions. No dead bodies, and no collections of comic books or baseball cards - just more books.

Our best work in the Elizabeth Public Library, and the reason we went there each afternoon, was to borrow our favorite books in a non-traditional way. Rich always wanted sci-fi and fantasy books. Ken had more varied tastes. And I stuck to the classics I would never read at thirteen but were important to have as I heard my grandfather say over and over: Dostoevski, Orwell, Stendhal, Hemingway, Dos Passos. We would take our books to the fourth floor and launch them out of a broken opened window in a forgotten corner of the library overlooking the back lot. You go there today and the lot is well lit. It is well-guarded and paved. Back in the 1980's it was a dark place where our books would fly out the window and land in the dust and sometimes in the mud of the parking lot. We would wait for the cover of darkness, 4:30 PM in a Jersey winter, and leave heading to the back lot to pick up our books and go home.

The three of us would laugh and joke all the way to my house happy with the books we wanted and happy to be twelve and thirteen the way only a boy that age can be when he is around other boys he knows are his friends. Sometimes one would pretend to kick the other in the head or plan the next sleepover so we could play Dungeons and Dragons well into the night. Sometimes we'd stop over at the Hunan Palace and share an .80 cent egg roll.

LESSONS FROM A TOUGH CROWD

On Elizabeth Avenue we sometimes did not have heat or the setting of the heat was too low. We did not control it. It was set downstairs by our landlords, the owners of the building, who owned Dan's Fine Furniture on the first floor. When the heat was set too low my mom would send me down to talk to Dan and his brother. In all the years we lived there I think I entered the furniture store fifty times and forty-nine times it was a heating issue.

"Mr. Fern. The heat."

"Hello. I don't know what more you want. It's turned on. Check the heaters." He would always respond.

"My mom says it's not working." I was just providing information and trying to stay neutral.

It smelled really good in his furniture store. It smelled of furniture we could not afford. I wondered if he would ever give us a deal on one of those nice leather couches. Dan Fern wondered why I was still hanging around looking at him sitting in his small office with a pencil in his hand and his glasses hanging off his nose.

He looked up at me. "Well, kid?"

"Thanks, Mr. Fern," I said.

"Is it cold up there? I mean, are you feeling cold?" He asked in a more apologetic tone.

"I don't know. My mom is cold," I answered.

I'd come upstairs and my mom would be screaming into the phone. "*Apúrate, muchacho.* Hurry! I caught a call to Cuba!" I'll have to explain that in those days to call Cuba you had to try over and over sometimes for hours, until magically you would "catch" a call and the number would start ringing at my grandmother's house in Havana. And it would ring and ring. And then Iris, my cousin the pianist, would pick it up.

"Oigo" literally means "I hear," which is how you answer the phone in Cuba.

"Iris. Iris. Iris. It's me. Lourdes and Fabio. How are you?"

"Lourdes!" she would scream back into the phone. Then promptly put the phone down and you could hear her running off screaming for my aunt, her mother, or my grandmother. She called her mother Beba. We all called her that. My grandmother was Pancha.

"Beba! Beba!" she hollered down the long hallway in my grandmother's house.

Then you'd wait and freak out because each minute was costing $1.29 or more. Beba would pick up the phone. Then my mom would let me talk to her. And then it would be a hand off and hand off like those plays you see sometimes in the final seconds of football games when you have a hard time figuring out who has the football and where it's going next. My grandmother would come on. Then back to Iris as she went to get Chela, my other aunt. Then Beba would get upset because Iris was asking us to send her aspirin and Vick's Vapor Rub and tea "when you send a package" or a letter. So Beba would be back, and then there would be a few agonizing minutes of hand offs asking emotional questions. It seemed they only wanted to ask about how much I was growing and tell me how they all missed me and how everyone in the neighborhood still asked about me. And then, about when my heart was going to be ripped open by the kindness poured through the phone in my grandmother's voice telling me to pray at night and never forget her or my grandfather, my dad would get the phone. He was quiet and calm as if he had just walked out of a shower and talcum powder. As if Cuba were Iceland and no one was in a hurry, my dad would come on the phone asking about school or what I was reading or about baseball. And I mixed resentment and pain and the pride of my pre-teen years and responded in one-word answers.

"Fine."

"ok."

"Bien."

"Sí."

"Bueno."

"Bye."

After the phone call, I'd walk back to my bedroom back on Elizabeth Avenue somewhat planted in the reality of New Jersey, but a part of me was still on the phone and in Cuba walking down the long hallway of my grandmother's house. I'd turn on the Atari or go back to playing Dungeons and Dragons with Ken and Rich. I'd be rolling the ten-sided dice so that my character could get past the orcs and find the treasure and the magic potions and the +2 sword.

Then would come the letters from Cuba. The ones from Iris were always identical. She had some kind of formula, like the letters of Saint Paul in the New Testament. Always start with a greeting. Then name as many family members as possible and ask you to give them a greeting. Then list other people who sent greetings. Then she would seamlessly shift to asking for things because they are needed. She mostly asked for medicines, but she would also throw in random items like a pair of boots or handkerchiefs or cash. Finally, she would give any bad news or good news. Deaths. Marriages. Births. Divorces. Funerals. Then she would close quickly, with a promise to write again. Those were Iris' letters. If you read one, I promise you, it's like you were reading all of them at once.

My grandmother had a different style. Her letters always began with the hope that "upon receiving these words, we were all being visited by good health and peace." Her letters flowed from story to story, but were never sentimental. I was her only grandson from her only son. And while I know she missed my presence, she never let it show. My grandmother, Tata, was old school. You suffer and you suffer in silence. My grandfather never wrote me letters that I can remember. He also never spoke to me on the phone. Where was he every time we called? He was good with numbers and math, could he not write? Did he not trust himself to be able to do what my grandmother did, to hold it all in and breathe and feel the voice on the phone and keep it all in and hold it all down?

Letters from Cuba took about a month and a half to arrive to us in New Jersey so they had to wish us Merry Christmas in mid-October or send a letter for my birthday around New Year's Eve. When they reached us in those old brown envelopes and written on brown paper I remember not wanting to read the letters. Better to watch TV and learn English and play football with my friends and go to "Kolker's" to buy "G.I. Joe" action figures and forget about Cuba.

I would rather have been riding my small BMX bike to Ken's house even at risk of getting jumped again when I turned left from Elizabeth Avenue onto Jacques Street by the corner pizzeria. Once near that corner a group of six or seven kids about my age saw me and chased me down to the middle of Ken's block. They wanted my bike. The lead kid, light-skinned and shirtless, stepped off his bike and stood in front of my handlebars straddling my front tire. First came the pretense of "nice bike" and "where you headed" and "oh yeah, we know that kid Ken." It's the sizing you up before you get jumped. You have to learn to watch for the small talk before the attack.

"Gimme your bike," he finally came out and grabbed the handle bar. "That's my brother's bike. You stole it from him."

I didn't bother defending myself. The kid knew this wasn't his brother's bike. His brother was probably old and serving jail time already. This was my bike. My bike in the United States and there was no way he was getting it. That was until he punched me hard square in the chest. Thud. First, I was surprised that he hit me. Then I knew he was going to hit me again, but I could not get off the bike. I also did not defend myself. I could have him hit him back. I should have. I just froze.

"Get off the bike you stupid Cuban!"

My legs were jelly and what he interpreted as defiance, I experienced as a complete meltdown with an inability to move. Minutes passed. For hours it seemed like I was standing there staring anywhere but in the kid's eyes.

"Just take his damn watch," he barked.

Another kid grabbed my watch and they took off.

I rode the rest of the half block to Ken's house and his mom opened the door smiling. Ken's mom had the kindness you just felt by being around her no matter what she said or didn't say. She'd give Ken "the blessing" right before he left the house to play or go to school. This meant making the sign of the cross on his forehead and saying a small prayer of protection. I'd walk in his house and sit on his bed.

"What's up, Fab?" He asked.

"Tough crowd today," I answered.

I should have told him that I talked to my father and my grandmother in Cuba and that we received letters from Cuba and that we did not have heat this morning, and that I got jumped and some kids took my watch. Instead, I just kept it all in and pushed it all down. I sat on his bed and made plans to play football in the street or baseball behind the closed-down school yard or call Rich at his mom's store to have him come over to Ken's house. But then Washington, our friend, not the President, would ring the doorbell and we'd go out on Jacques Street and play football, two-hand touch, and I'd forget about Cuba, for a while.

PLAYING BASEBALL WITH MY GRANDFATHER

My grandfather smelled like a pipe. Not a burnt-out bad pipe smell, nor the smell of exhaust out of motorcycle pipes, nor like a sewer pipe. No, I mean like a smoking pipe. It was a mixed smell of something hard and strong mixed with something deep and pleasant. He lived with us for a few years on Elizabeth Avenue, mostly when I was still twelve and thirteen. His room was the little room at the very front of the apartment, just to the left of the front door and off the kitchen/dining room area. A few years later I took that room because my cousin Sara and baby Marla came from Cuba and we gave them my bigger room on the opposite end of the apartment, facing Elizabeth Avenue. This room had a window that opened onto the street and the Salvation Army across from it. And so my grandfather's room became my room.

Alberto Martinez Herrera, my grandfather, was born on July 2 in Cienfuegos, Cuba. He always lied about his age so I will honor that and omit his birth year. When my grandfather lived in our apartment he kept his little room organized. He was a man of rituals. The green typewriter sat at a small desk just so and next to it were a pen and his pipe and a handkerchief. There may also have been a small cup where he kept water or beer, depending on the day and the mood. His bed was always made. He had few clothes, including a hat that made him look like Humphrey Bogart. He would have loved that reference. He also kept a strict schedule about reading, and he would sit in a rocking chair for hours with novels borrowed from the local libraries. He woke early and read in the morning for hours. He also wrote. In fact, his memoir is still one of my "go-to" books when I want to hear his irreverent humor, his satire, and his love of life.

I spent a lot of time with him in the early 90's when I was in my early twenties. He sent me many letters wherever all of my crazy adventures took me during those tumultuous years: Kingwood, West Virginia; Cincinnati, Ohio; Baltimore, Maryland; Scranton, Pennsylvania; Miami, Florida, and back to Elizabeth. He was a faithful correspondent and would send me tapes he'd record of himself reading the short stories he was writing. But in my early pre-teen years our conversations were mostly like this:

"Hey. Abuelo," I would interrupt his reading.

"What?" He'd ask, annoyed at my interruption.

"What are you doing?" I asked.

"Reading, *chico*. Can't you see? They did give you eyes, right?"

I wouldn't stop with my questions. "When will you finish?"

"*Amigo mío*," he'd elongate those words and sometimes repeat them in a different cadence. "Why don't *you* go read a book instead of playing Atari all day or that stupid dungeons y *dragones* game that you play? Doesn't this generation read?"

"I need to go to "Kolker's" and *Mami* won't let me walk there alone. Will you take me?" I finally asked.

"Ah, so you want me to go with you? *Está bien*. But when we are walking together, don't call me *abuelo* in public."

"Hmmm? What do you mean?" I did not understand his demand.

He explained in detail that he did not want anyone to think he was that old. "Call me uncle."

"Ok, *abuelo*, but will you take me?" I repeated.

"Sí, let's go." He would finally grant my request.

In his little room, he would also spend time in front of his old typewriter working on stories or articles to publish or on letters he was writing. If my English-speaking friends called he'd tell them on the phone that I went "boiling" instead of bowling. It made for interesting follow-up conversations.

For the span of about a year he joined Tan and me in playing a tabletop baseball game that Tan had made me, using a piece of flat wood with drilled holes. We used a marble, as a baseball, and a marker, as a bat. We played an entire season among three teams with big league players we drafted. We kept box scores and stats and knew who led our league in home runs and base hits and strikeouts and innings pitched. It was fantasy baseball before any such thing existed. And I took it so seriously.

I remember that my ace pitcher was Fernando Valenzuela. I could only have him pitch once every four or five games because we wanted to keep the game realistic and pitchers need the rest between games. It just so happened that my grandfather's team was playing my team toward the end of a season and Valenzuela was pitching looking for his league-leading win and ERA (earned run average.) That day, Valenzuela got rocked by my grandfather's team. After three innings, he had already scored three runs, but I kept him in the game, and in the bottom of the fifth my grandfather started scoring and scoring runs. Instead of pulling my ace pitcher, I stubbornly kept him on the mound because I was shell-shocked. The more runs my grandfather's team scored the more I wanted to punish Valenzuela by keeping him on the mound.

My dad had to stop the game after Valenzuela had given up about seven runs in one inning to remind me that ERA would skyrocket if I did not pull him from the game. Instead, I ran off to the bathroom and cried. This wailing was so embarrassing as a twelve-year-old. Crying over a baseball game and only because I could not stand to lose and especially to my grandfather who did not know Valenzuela nor anything about baseball. How could I beat my dad, but lose to my grandfather?

Of course, the game required the "skill" of the person hitting the marble with the marker, aiming the hit for the drilled holes that were color-coded to indicate a hit, or a double, a home run, or an out. For me, this baseball game my dad had built me was the absolutely coolest game of my childhood, even ahead of video games and Risk. It was also a game I shared with my dad. So, it seemed unjust to lose to my grandfather who knew *nothing* about baseball while I knew every player in the 1984 N.Y. Mets roster. And my grandfather did not make losing easier.

"That Valenzuela. Valentino. Vacaccino. Whatever his name is. *Amigo mío*, he won't even have what the chickens have left to eat."

"Hmmm," I tried containing my anger.

"Let's do this. Let's erase some runs so that Valenzuela can keep his manhood."

"Hmmm. Hmmmm." I tried to hold my cool.

"Don't get discouraged, Fabio. Next season might be better for you"

"I am going to kill you. I hate you!" I would yell at him losing control.

"Whatever. Just don't call me *abuelo* in public."

MY AUNT, PANAMA, AND JULIO IGLESIAS

When I was about twelve, my aunt, Marucha managed to find a way out of Cuba along with Edmundo Castillo, her husband, my uncle. They were able to leave the same day within a few hours of each other. One catch. He wound up in Panama. She ended up in New Jersey. She had been able to reestablish her residency in the U.S. from when as a child she lived in Hoboken in the late 1950's. He could not since they were not married at that time when she was twelve. It was my father who took them to the airport and then stayed with my aunt during the hours after Castillo, my uncle, flew out and her flight left. He waited with her and then stood on the airport terrace waving goodbye as she walked to her plane. She flew to Miami and then to New Jersey. We took her in; that's what family does. She lived with us on Elizabeth Avenue, in our cramped apartment. And for the first time since he had left Cuba, my grandfather had both daughters in New Jersey.

My aunt loved Julio Iglesias. You may have heard of Julio Iglesias because he sang songs with Willie Nelson. You may have heard of Willie Nelson because he sang "On the Road Again," a classic. She played Julio songs all day long. I mostly remember her around the house singing and dancing to "Hey". Loosely translated from the Spanish version the song goes like this:

Hey! Don't go walking around
saying I can't live without you.
I know you like to tell your friends I can't live without you.
Don't think you help yourself
when you tell people about my love for you and make fun of me.
Hey! It's better to love than be loved and not be capable of feeling
what I feel for you.
You see.
You've never loved me.

And so on. You get the idea. The irony is that she could not live without my uncle and after a few months alone in New Jersey she wanted to fly down to Panama City to join him. That was clearly not the original plan. The idea was for both to be in the USA in *La Yuma*. She would call him in Panama City to the boarding home where he lived. "Pachi. Ay, Pachi." She called him "Pachi." I have never figured out what that was short for because there is not a longer word in Spanish I can associate with it. Just a term of endearment, I guess.

"Marucha, please be rational. Be calm." My uncle called her what we all called my aunt. She was Maria Teresa by birth name, but I never heard any one call her anything other than Marucha. You can see the association with María.

"No, Pachi. No. I can't stand it. I have to see you. They are making my life impossible here," she begged.

"Marucha. Think. Think. Calm. Please. In less than a year I'll have the visa and be with you there and we'll save some money. You see. I have done all the calculations.," he said reassuringly.

The heart does not know about rational calculations. My grandfather was behind the scenes smoking his pipe, sitting in his long underwear in his rocking chair, with a book and small glass of beer at his side. "I don't trust any Cuban man alone. For a whole year? A whole year? Alone. Not even a Cuban mathematician."

"But Marucha, my love, my little piece of sky (all corny, even in Spanish), my little angel. We must think."

"A year? Ay, no. No, Pachi. *Me voy*. I am going. There with you. With you." She continued to insist.

"That doesn't make sense, Marucha. Talk to Alberto and he'll make you understand." My uncle wouldn't give in to her pleas.

She had been talking to Julio Iglesias.

I sat in my small room and listened in to their phone conversation, my dog Katia on my lap. Is she going to leave to go to Panama? That made no sense to me. Why would you leave the country that we are all trying to get to? You have to do things that make sense. Look at my father in Cuba. When my mom asked him to sign over a legal document saying he would allow me to leave the country, he signed it. Because it made sense.

Because in *la USA* I could fully develop and become so many great things professionally and personally. He explained this to me in a letter, in 1989 when I was eighteen. This is why he had not left Cuba and why he let me go. I keep that letter on my desk even to this day. It would have made no sense to refuse and to keep me in Cuba growing up in a Communist country, with all the limitations of thought and of personal and political freedom. How does my aunt not see that?

"*Mejor juntos, Pachi.* Together." She would not give up.

"But Marucha I don't have any money here and it will be harder taking care of you here and this house is cramped and some days food."

She cut in. "I don't care, Pachi. *Together.*"

I think often about the decision I would make in my father's shoes if I were asked what my mother asked him to sign. I am not proud of it, but the answer would be "No Way, José! I am not signing anything that places my children thousands of miles and another galaxy away from me." It's selfish what my aunt decided to do. But I'd do the same. And for years I have wondered what great strength or great weakness allowed my father to do the opposite. I don't have a good answer yet, but separation from the person you love is the most difficult trial of all. It's why the concept of Hell in Catholic theology is simply defined as the only place where God is not present. That is what makes it a torture, the lack of the presence of God. The separation. It's why death is so painful even though "we believe in the communion of saints, the forgiveness of sins, the resurrection of the body, and life everlasting. Amen."

And she left the "*La Yuma.*" Out of Paradise. And into paradise.

Marucha and Pachi went through a difficult time down there for about nine months. No money. A lousy low paying job for Castillo, who was a math teacher by trade. Some tutoring gig to make side money. They don't talk much now about all they suffered together. Eventually, they both made it out of Panama and returned to New Jersey where Castillo worked for years as a math teacher and they happily grew old together.

"But what about me?" I wondered.

What about you kid? An imaginary voice asked.

"Well. Was it right? My separation from Cuba? From my father?"

Come on, kid? Look around? What do you think? Better yet, what does your heart say? You wanna go back and stay in Cuba? Do it over that way and see what sticks?

"No way José!" I screamed internally.

DREAMING IN ENGLISH

"The past is never dead. It's not even past."
William Faulkner

"I can fix a lot of things but um, this one's all yours..."
Arthur "Fonzie" Fonzarelli

I don't know the exact day it happened. I wish I could say February 6th or May 19th. It happened after years of *Little House on the Prairie* and *Happy Days* and Saturday morning cartoons, when Saturdays were the only time a kid could watch cartoons on television. It was a day after years of friendship with Ken and Rich and the sleepovers at Rich's house in Hillside. One day I woke up and I realized I had just had a dream, in English.

"Why is that such a big deal?" Ken would ask. His parents spoke to him in Spanish, but since he was born in Summit, New Jersey, he did all his dreaming in English.

"It means I can speak English. I'm *thinking* in English." I said excitedly.

"Yeah, but you are thinking about Cuba," Ken replied.

"No, I am not thinking about Cuba at all."

If there had been a movie camera I would have looked into it and narrated that in those early years in New Jersey I did not think much about Cuba because I was busy forgetting it in order to learn the United States. I wanted to be Fonzie from *Happy Days* and he was far from Cuban. I wanted to play football with the Miami Dolphins and Dan Marino or baseball with the New York Mets and Dwight Gooden. I wanted to be more American than Americans and my definition of American was pretty narrow at twelve.

All narrators want to be honest and so far I have tried to tell you an honest story. But here I want to dream about sitting down in the same room on Elizabeth Avenue, in the small living room of that apartment, during a Christmas morning, with all the people that were already in my life story at age twelve. It was a small living room with wooden sliding doors that closed off the two bedrooms, a gray couch, a small 21-inch television, and a lazy-boy chair; it would be a tight fit in that room.

In this dream, it would have been frigid cold outside that afternoon and the streets had fresh snow. I could see a puny snowman below on Elizabeth Avenue. An old man shuffled by the snowman with some small pieces of glass in his hands. I saw my mom coming home from Foodtown Supermarket where she went every afternoon. She would be shocked to find so many relatives in her living room. My grandfather would sit on the rocking chair reading Stendhal or Faulkner. He would come out of his room hearing the noise of Tan, my stepdad, making tortillas and talking loudly to three Kings from the Orient.

Then in the living room everyone else gathered. And one by one I could talk to them or just look at them one more time. First, the Cuban family would have a turn: My grandmother, Tata, with her bony hands, would hold my face just so and I could fall asleep on her shoulder and hug her tight. We'd pray a Hail Mary and sing a *bolero* together. I know the one:

Aquellos ojos verdes
De mirada serena
Dejaron en mi alma
Eterna fe de amar

Those green eyes
With their calm look
Leave in my soul
The eternal faith of love.

Anhelos de caricias
De besos y ternuras
De todas las dulzuras
Que han podido brindar

Yearning for caresses,
Kisses and tenderness

Like all of the sweetness
They were able to offer me.

Aquellos ojos verdes
Serenos como un lago
En cuyas quietas aguas
Un día me miré

Those green eyes
Calm like a lake
In their quiet waters
One day I saw myself

No saben la tristeza
Que en mi alma dejaron
Aquellos ojos verdes
Que nunca olvidaré

They don't know the sadness
That they left in my soul
Those green eyes
I will never forget.

My paternal grandfather Rogelio, who had stayed in Cuba, and I would talk about baseball and my future girlfriends and he'd tell me how to be upright and honest and always a good man. I would drink a glass of milk with him. I would introduce him to my maternal grandfather Alberto, who lived with us in Elizabeth, as if the two had never met. You can't think of two people more different in temperament. And I would ask them what they were thinking trying to both co-exist inside me.

I would talk to both together. "How is it possible I could be both you and you? Hold on. Before you answer that. One of you is calm and rational and courteous to women and small animals. And then there is you, abuelo. Well. You are…"

"*¿Amigo mío...para qué, tú crees que te necesitamos?*" (My friend, why do you think we need you?) my New Jersey grandfather would ask.

"I have no idea why you need me in this story, abuelo," I replied.

"You needed both of us to tell your story. Just like you'll need both Cuba and New Jersey. And we both," he would point to my other grandfather, "need *you* to tell our story."

"Oh. Wow!" I'd reply, paralyzed by the idea.

"These Americans! All they know how to say at anything is "wow," my grandfather would say. "Like children!"

"Yeah. I did not realize that. But of course, I am *twelve*. How could I?" I thought.

"You are a doofus. Now, Lucky for you, I'll spend a lot of time talking with you in your late teens and early twenties and that will shape your understanding of life. And you'll read Dostoevski. If not for those two things, ahhh," my grandfather concluded taking a puff of his Dr. Grabow pipe.

"Thanks, abuelo," I said gratefully.

My other grandfather would step in to defend me. "Alberto, the child is no doofus. One day he will be a man and a father and a grandfather."

"But I won't get to hear from you on that, abuelo, And I never got to ride the Lenin Park ponies without you holding the reins," I'd say to my Cuba grandfather.

"You won't need to. You already have. I have already filled you with what you will one day need. My love for you. Lenin Park. Riding the ponies. Me holding the reins. *Always*. You trusting and riding the pony. That is all you need to know."

"Wow!" I was overwhelmed.

"And there he goes again. You say he is no doofus, but all he's got is *Wow* and *Wow*. We may be pinning our hopes on the wrong kid. I have a lot of work to do with this boy." My grandfather remarked punctuating the statement with his pipe.

"I get it! I am going to forget these things for years, but when I need them, they'll be there and back again," I realized.

"Yes, we will." In my dream, they both say this in unison. *It could hap-*

pen. It is, after all, a dream.

"Wow!" I repeated.

"That's how it works muchacho. Don't be such a doofus!"

Then my grandfather with blue-green eyes would look at my grandfather with the pipe and they would compare notes on their opposite and similar lives, one an immigrant in New Jersey and the other back in Cuba. Then the silence would break with my cousin Iris playing the piano and screaming at me and I'd laugh and cry at the same time. My great-aunts, Beba and Chela, could talk to me about how as a kid I was such a good egg. And I would want to listen to the radio with my Tio Alberto, especially the 1976 U.S. presidential elections, if possible.

Buried in time is the suggestion that time is not buried at all. That at any moment you could say something and bring it all in and all back. If you are Cuban-American that sensation haunts you and you are somehow always obsessed with the past. Find out how many Cuban-Americans have become physicists, theologians, or poets: all battling time. I'd love to know. And for a long time I feared this about memories and time. That they could come back and do harm. I am trusting in you to tell me that they won't.

MASS, TEA, KATE, AND SWALLOW

"Are we going to Mass?" she asked. "I think my sister Kate will be there," she added.

"Can you make iced tea?" I rolled over in bed.

She picked up a postcard from my bookshelf. The bookshelf my stepdad had built with the gray bricks and planks of varnished wood. The postcard was a flock of flying birds.

"The swallows. So beautiful. Do they fly South for the winter? No, I am serious. I don't know anything about birds. Am I supposed to know?"

"Make tea. Please. I just had the strangest feeling." I paused because I was back in Cuba. I was a child. I was back in Lawton and Vibora Park. "This moment and you saying that, reminded me of Cuba."

"Everything reminds you of Cuba," she said and smiled.

EPILOGUE AND OTHER WORKS

I want to suggest a few other books you can read to remain human in a world constantly pushing you in the opposite direction. These are the "books" that have broken and healed my heart. Some of these, maybe I loved only because I am an immigrant, and will always remain half of something and half of another thing. But, maybe that has value for you. As humans, we all tend to be half this and half that anyway. Some of them you will have to wait a year or five or twenty to read, but a few you can pick up right now and read in your teenage years.

You will have other books, but I wanted you to have **my list**.

Red Scarf Girl, Ji-Li Liang. The memoir of a childhood marked by the Cultural Revolution in China. You will understand what Communism means after you read this book which is good for both kids and adults.

The Hobbit, J.R.R. Tolkien. Because I always wanted to be a hobbit! He is, after all, like me, a little guy in a strange land. Not the movies, though. Read the novel.

Casablanca, the film. Because love does find a way.

The Little House on the Prairie series. I am not ashamed to admit I learned to speak English a great deal thanks to Laura Ingalls Wilder, her books, and this show.

George Orwell's *1984,* and *Animal Farm* because both should be required reading since our humanity is under threat.

Mere Christianity, C.S. Lewis. Because you have to know the offer before you can accept it or decline it. My life would have been meaningless without this understanding. This book by Jack probably saved me. Read it.

Carlos Eire has two books on growing up in Cuba: *Waiting for Snow in Havana* and *Learning to Die in Miami.* He is of my parent's generation. Must read to understand the anguish and the beauty of being Cuban.

Finding Mañana, Mirta Ojito. This is the Mariel Boatlift. Well-written and explained.

The philosopher and theologian Peter Kreeft claims there are six books that will save Western Civilization: *Lost in the Cosmos,* Walker Percy,

The Abolition of Man, and *Mere Christianity,* C.S. Lewis, *The Everlasting Man* and *Orthodoxy,* by G.K. Chesterton, and *Brave New World,* Aldous Huxley. All must be read to understand what it means to be a person. I love them all.

A Severe Mercy, Sheldon Vanauken. Because we never say goodbye and conversions happen. One of my early favorites when I became a believer.

William Faulkner's Nobel Prize acceptance speech. Because if you have grown up in the South, Faulkner should be required reading. I will also place Faulkner's *The Sound and the Fury* and *The Unvanquished* on this list.

All the King's Men, Robert Penn Warren. As true now as it was 75 years ago.

Fides et Ratio (Faith and Reason), the encyclical by John Paul II. Because those who pit faith against reason do not understand reason and have not lived the faith. Don't fall for that trap. Read JPII.

The novels of Walker Percy as well as *Lost in the Cosmos.*

The Return of the Prodigal Son by Henri Nouwen. Forgiveness.

The short stories of Ernest Hemingway and *The Old Man and the Sea.*

And Dostoyevsky's *The Brothers Karamazov* and *Crime and Punishment.*

ACKNOWLEDGEMENTS

"When a person doesn't have gratitude, something is missing in his or her humanity. A person can almost be defined by his or her attitude toward gratitude."
Elie Wiesel

I owe a debt of eternal gratitude for making this book possible:

to Roberto Madrigal, and Termino Editorial, for agreeing to take this flawed work and publish it. But to Roberto, I owe the greater debt of taking me in when I was 17 and a freshman at Xavier University, and giving me an equal share of the blessings of his home. I owe Marta and Nicole and Freeway for teaching me how to do dishes and wait for Cuban coffee and for trips to used bookstores and gathering leaves and all that is a beautiful in Cincinnati, Ohio and in life.

to Kistin Jordan of Kistin Creative Studios for her creative genius and willingness to take on this project and for the cover of this book and for her patience and kindness to take on my little project as if it were her most important one.

to my first editor Stephen Wildfeuer for his courage to be firm when it was needed and the grace to tell me I had to publish these stories. Stephen was the first non-family member who read this complete text and without him and his detailed love of this manuscript this work would have been lost. So much of him shaped the prose and my debt to him is the size of an hippopotame.

to Claudia Velandia, who while at home recovering from surgery agreed to read the manuscript and edit the parts in Spanish.

to the 7th grade class at Cannon School in October 2017 for being the first group of students who listened to two stories from this collection.

to my daughters Rebecca and Grace who read the first complete version and loved it, perhaps only because their dad had written it. That was all I needed to press on with all my heart.

to my daughter Elisa, and my sons Francis and Matthew, who taught me, as they grew up, that if you do not lose hope and do not despair, even when it is darkest, you earn the rewards that God has prepared in your tomorrows.

to my son Joseph who read the first story in an email I sent him and then kept asking for one more story one email at a time. Giving me hope since April 5, 2002. You the real MVP!

to my employment at Archbishop Curley Notre Dame High School (ACND) from 1998 to 2004 because it was during final exam proctoring one year that while standing at a podium for three hours proctoring a Biology exam, I started writing this book. I also owe ACND because my oldest daughter Krystin is an alumna, and her education at ACND prepared her for marriage, motherhood, law school, and life. And because there I was part of the finest group of faculty members I have ever seen assembled. No need for names. You know who you are.

to Ken, Rich, John, Jason, and Geronimo who taught me about friendship even when I did not know how to fully be a friend. Forever grateful and thinking of you every day.

to the best teacher I have known, Mr. Jacque Leighty, who opened truth, beauty, goodness, and commitment in the pages of Plato's "Allegory of the Cave" so that we could commune with it.

to my family who fill these pages. I love you far beyond the boundaries of the words I sometimes forget to say.

most essentially to my mother, because this is, in many ways, also her story, a telling of her life. And because her strength, courage, and love saved me and our family.

to the communion of saints who prayed this into existence.

And to my wife who loved each story as I have read it to her, and in whose beautiful eyes I saw myself one Christmas Eve twenty years ago and with whom I live the truest love story that God has written with our lives.

ABOUT THE AUTHOR

FABIO Alberto Hurtado was born in La Habana, Cuba at Hijas de Galicia Hospital in February 1971. He attended Cuban schools until 5th grade and left Cuba in September of 1980. After three months in Costa Rica, Fabio, his mother, and step-father moved to the United States and settled in Elizabeth, New Jersey.

Fabio has a B.A. in English, Philosophy, and Religion from Kean University and an M.A. in Theology from Holy Apostles Seminary. His first year as an educator came in 1994-1995 as a 4th grade teacher in Baltimore. He has been an educator for 23 years with experience in middle school and high school classrooms as an English, Spanish, and Theology teacher.

Since 2008 Fabio has been a teacher and administrator at Cannon School, an independent school in Concord, North Carolina.

Fabio is married to Teresita and has seven children and three grandchildren. Contact the author at fabhurt71@gmail.com